5-5-03

To Warren

MW01615102

May you enjoy "Buckets" of Success!

Best Wishes

Ray Lam

BUCKETS OF MONEY®

How to Retire in Comfort and Safety

BUCKETS OF MONEY®

How to Retire in Comfort and Safety

Raymond J. Lucia, CFP™
with Dale Fetherling

BrainTrust Publishing
San Diego, California

Cover design: Lorilee Art Services
Composition and art: Thompson Type
Photos: Professional Photographic Services

Please Note:

The examples and results shown in this book are for illustration only. Results are not guaranteed, and your results may vary by a considerable degree. A number of factors—including the overall economy, the financial markets, and the performance of your particular investments—can affect your results.

In giving these examples, we do not promise or predict any specific outcome. All investments involve risk, and any investment strategy can produce losses as well as gains, including loss of principal invested.

Buckets of Money® is a registered mark of The Raymond J. Lucia Companies, Inc. and may not be used in any manner whatsoever without written permission.

Dedication

To my wife Jeanne, my best friend and soul mate for over 30 years. She is a pillar of strength who has patiently stood by me, tolerating my crazy schedule of radio, television, client work, and study. Thank you for allowing me the time to write this book and pursue my passion.

To my children—Alana, Ray Jr., Dom, and Niki—who have been the joy of my life and a great inspiration. I couldn't be more proud.

To my mom and dad, who not only fed me well (a little *too* well, actually) but gave me a true sense of values and taught me that family, not money, is the most important thing.

To my brother Michael Lucia, ChFC, a terrific financial advisor whose dedication and work with clients has helped and motivated me immensely.

To my staff of financial and personal advisors—including Melissa Dotson, Rick Plum, CFP™, Rob Butterfield, J.D., Marc Seward, ChFC, and the rest of my team with whom I work and learn from each day.

And to the almost 2,000 clients who are using the *Buckets of Money*® strategy. They have entrusted me and my firm with their money, a responsibility we take very seriously. And it is because of them and people just like them that I have written this book.

A Special Note

When I began writing this book we were well into the middle of the greatest boom in stock market history. Talking about safe money for income, reasonably safe money for "tomorrow," along with a modest allocation to equities and real estate, wasn't very popular. Everyone was making big bucks on their individual stock bets, high-tech mutual funds, dot-com IPOs, day trading, and the like.

But by mid-March 2000, a brutal bear market was born. Who would have thought that many stalwart companies like Cisco Systems, Sun Microsystems, Oracle, and even Home Depot, Microsoft, Disney, and General Electric would lose up to 80% of their value? Then on September 11, 2001, the country was shocked and appalled when terrorists attacked America by flying hijacked jetliners into the World Trade Center towers in New York and into the Pentagon in Washington, D.C. This further roiled the financial markets.

Anyone invested in the stock market since March, 2000 has been hurt financially by the bursting of the tech bubble, which then was compounded by this terrorist tragedy. But despite the short-term impact on the stock market and the toll such events take on consumer confidence, the U.S. economy is still quite resilient, and stocks will one day return to become respectable investments. Because no one can forecast tragedy or its effect on the financial markets, it is even more critical that individuals have their Buckets of Money® set up properly.

We know that time mitigates risk, and Buckets will help you do that. But while neither Buckets of Money® nor a soaring bull market could ever cause us to forget those who innocently lost their lives on that tragic day, the events of the last couple of years do help us to understand the importance of planning. I hope this book will motivate you to do just that.

—R.J.L.

Note on tax rates

Reduced tax rates are a centerpiece of the federal Taxpayer Relief Act of 2001. But the cuts are phased in gradually and the full effect won't be felt until 2006.

For example, the highest individual rate of 39.6% in 2000 will decrease to 39.1% in 2001, 38.6% in 2002 and on down until it reaches 35% in 2006. Similarly the 28% tax rate eventually will become 25%, and a new 10% bracket will be added, though the 15% bracket will be unchanged.

This presents a problem for this book because most tax-rate figures would be obsolete by the time you read them.

So, in the interest of sanity and clarity, we have stuck with the 2000 rates—generally 39.6%, 28%, and 15%—in our examples. But the same planning principles will apply, and you can choose to mentally reduce slightly many of the tax rates mentioned in the examples.

TABLE OF CONTENTS

UNDERSTANDING THE BUCKETS

FILLING THE BUCKETS

'BUCKETIZING' YOUR LIFE

LIVING HAPPILY EVER AFTER AS A BUCKETEER

Preface

What 'Buckets' Can Mean for You

O.K., right off the bat, here's a pop quiz (but it's an easy one).

Are you:

	Yes	No
• Retired?	___	___
• Thinking about retiring?	___	___
• Starting to worry about whether you'll have enough money to retire?	___	___
• Managing your own money?	___	___
• Disturbed by the stock market's sometimes violent swings?	___	___
• Concerned about inflation eating away at the purchasing power of the money you worked so long and hard for?	___	___

Well, if you answered "yes" to any of those questions, you can profit from the *Buckets of Money*® strategy. In short, it's a way of *generating steady income while still taking advantage of the historically-proven growth in stocks and other long-term investments.*

That's not doublespeak: Achieving both goals—income and growth—is not only do-able, it's a smart and conservative way to protect *and* grow your nest egg. In fact, in more than 28 years as a financial planner and as a manager of what's now more than a half a billion dollars in assets, I have found nothing as simple—and as powerful—as this concept.

But, first, let me be clear about what *Buckets of Money*® is *not*. It's not a get-rich-quick scheme. It won't make you as fabulously wealthy as if you'd invested big time in Microsoft 25 years ago. (You missed that opportunity, huh? So did I.) *Buckets of Money*® doesn't involve some high-wire act like futures trading, currency arbitrage, penny stocks, or dealing in distressed real estate. You don't have to predict the future and you won't need to raise chinchillas, plant jojobas, or be atop the crest of some so-called technological wave of the future.

All you need to do is know your financial goals, divvy up your money accordingly, and then invest intelligently, according to guidelines I'm going to give you in this book. It's a conservative—but growth-oriented—strategy that hopefully will allow you to:

- Live comfortably in retirement without having to work (though you may choose to.)
- Sleep well at night without worrying about your money running out.

Let me hasten to add, *Buckets of Money*® is not a plan without risk—*no* investment is ever totally risk-free. How the overall economy fares, the way the financial markets perform, and the ups and downs of your particular investments will affect the results you get. We do not predict any specific outcome.

But having said that, let me tell you that this is a sound way to reduce risk while still taking advantage of growth. What's more, I know hundreds, perhaps thousands, of people, probably very much like you, who have used the *Buckets of Money*® principle to build and enjoy a financially comfortable retirement.

Sad to say, I've also seen many people begin their retirement thinking they had enough money to live on for the rest of their lives. But the twin dangers—inflation and taxes—ate away at their financial cushion until they either had to cut back drastically on their standard of living or go back to work just to survive. Sometimes they depleted their estates so much that the legacy they hoped to leave for their children was but a fraction of what they intended. Please, *don't* let that happen to you.

Speaking bluntly

To put it bluntly, the object of financial planning for retirement is to avoid running out of money before you run out of time. And the focus of the *Buckets of Money*® strategy is taking advantage of the long-term potential of stocks and other equity-type investments while securing a safe, predictable income from assets. It's especially appropriate for retirees and those looking to enhance income while reducing risk. However, the Buckets principle works for everyone, regardless of age, income, net worth, or investment experience.

In brief, here's how it operates: You put your money into three "buckets" and invest each in a different way. (As you become a more informed Bucketeer, you'll find that from time to time you may need more than three buckets because some will hold pre-tax money, some post-tax cash, etc. But for the sake of simplicity, let's just talk for now about the three main buckets.) The cash deposited in Bucket No. 1 goes into very safe, low-growth vehicles like CDs, money markets, Treasury instruments, and short-term bonds. Using both principal and interest, Bucket No. 1 provides a safe income stream that you can live off for a specified number of years. (Don't panic at the thought of spending both principal and interest. You'll see later why we totally deplete Bucket No. 1.)

Meanwhile, your Bucket No. 2 is growing. This bucket, depending on your tolerance for risk, may be invested in slightly more aggressive investments with better potential for returns. After Bucket No. 1 is empty, you pour money from your Bucket No. 2 into Bucket No. 1 for yet another specified period of years.

By the time Bucket No. 1 is again depleted, Bucket No. 3—full of stocks and similar high-growth investments—will have had all that time to grow and with any kind of luck at all, you'll then have a nice chunk of change to see you through your sunset years. While Bucket No. 3 is more risky, that risk is mitigated by time. So if Buckets Nos. 1 and 2 last 12 to 14 years that should provide an ample cushion in the event the stock market takes a short-term dive requiring a few months or even a few years to recover.

That's the short course. Naturally, there are lots of variations, such as how much you put in each bucket, how long you let it grow, and the kinds of investments that are right for each bucket. We'll go into all that as well as how to make sure that you're covered for emergencies that may pop up.

Among the big plusses of Buckets is its simplicity. Even a rookie investor can understand and make use of the basic philosophy. Another advantage is that Buckets is flexible enough for the more sophisticated investor, that person who likes to get every last one-quarter of a percentage point of return and who seemingly follows the financial markets with a magnifying glass. Further, you can modify your Buckets program as your situation changes. If you get a windfall, or you need more cash to live on, or you want to increase or decrease your potential return and your exposure to risk, the strategy is easy to alter.

So . . . relax and enjoy this book. I've tried to make it as simple and clear as possible. Believing that an ounce of application is worth a ton of abstraction, I've used plenty of examples and have sought to avoid financial gobbledegook.

As you learn about this strategy, think about your goals and how you might adapt the Buckets program for your situation. Keep in mind, too, that there are no perfect solutions, no absolute answers, no right and no wrong ways to invest. Each person's investment objective, comfort level, risk tolerance, and tax situation will determine the best investment choices to fill each bucket.

What do I know?

Having been a financial planner since 1974, I've seen good times and bad. For almost 11 years I've also fielded thousands of money questions on my nationally-syndicated radio talk show and responded to a flood of emails and letters. I've studied the financial markets and have seen interest rates at 18% and 6% and everywhere in between. I have watched the real-estate roller coaster create moguls and paupers. I've seen quick-buck artists come and go (sometimes to jail.) I've seen salesmen so slick they could sell a stethoscope to a tree surgeon, yet didn't have the slightest idea of what they were talking about.

I've seen it all, and this is what I've learned: You've got to analyze your particular situation. Then you've got to allocate your assets in a way that's smart and sound. This takes patience and some wisdom, too.

The wisdom part, which I'll discuss in the last chapter, means knowing that money, as important as it is, is not the object of the game. Playing a good game is the object of the game. Speaking of games, I once heard someone describe a perfect football player: Smart enough to understand the plays and dumb enough to think they're important. I'd propose a variation of that for the perfect investor: Smart enough to know how money works but not dumb enough to think that's only what life is all about.

What does money represent in your life? A necessary means to an end, or an end in itself? Hold that thought. We'll get back to that.

How this book works

A few words about how this book is organized. The first two chapters give the big picture on handling your money long-term. In essence, because nobody is smart enough to predict what will happen to the economy next year or even five years from now, an intelligent asset-allocation program is your best bet for being able to meet rising costs without worry.

After exploring your tolerance for risk and explaining the Buckets principle in more detail, the next three sections (Chapters 5 through 7) tell how to choose the best investments for each bucket and also go into some of the tax issues. The next two chapters suggest how to tweak the buckets in special situations, regardless of the kind of retirement savings—401(k), Keogh, IRA, Roth IRA, CDs, etc.—that you may have.

Chapters 10 and 11 give some pointers on how to find a financial planner and what other steps to take to put your finances on a sound path. Lastly, Chapter 12 includes a bit of wit and wisdom, for whatever it's worth. In the appendices, you'll find a list of other books and resources I think you might enjoy and profit from.

This book will teach you the basics of bucket planning and bucket filling. If you carefully follow the strategies discussed you will become a master Bucketeer, and, I truly hope, live a financially fulfilling life!

A product of many hands

This book is a product of many hands. My sincere thanks go to all who contributed to it, especially Rob Butterfield Jr., Esq.; Rick Plum, CFP™; Michael Lucia, ChFC; Marc Seward, ChFC; Melissa Dotson; Ray Lucia Jr.; Lyn Rowe, CFP™; Janean Stripe, CFP™; John Dean; Bill Izor, CFP™, CLU, ChFC; Ryan Bowers; Susan Macy; Mike Sztrom; LuAnn Porter; Dale Fetherling; Paul Kosmos; and Mike Smith, MBA, Ph.D.

Chapter 1

EVERYBODY'S GOT AN INVESTMENT IDEA— BUT IS IT A *GOOD* IDEA?

If there's anything we've got plenty of in our Information Age, it's advice about how to make a bundle. Money gurus promise wealth without risk. Financial magazines trumpet the latest trends. The Internet virtually bristles with offers. Our neighbors or co-workers eagerly share their astounding stock-market secrets. And the daily mail overflows with wealth-building tips.

As a result, many of us are surrounded by opportunities, flooded with information—*much of it wrong*—and often totally confused about how to build a nest egg so we can enjoy a decent retirement.

But, actually, what most people want to know is simply:

- How can I retire in reasonable comfort?
- How can I know my retirement funds will keep pace with inflation and taxes?

- How can I protect myself from the short-term swings in the stock and bond markets?

Those are increasingly urgent questions for an astounding number of people. Here's a startling statistic: The number of Americans 65 and older will grow almost five times faster over the next 40 years than those in the 20–64 age group. What that means is that tens of millions of workers—far more than in any other era in our history—will soon reach the end of their working lives. So "How can I retire successfully?" is a question that's quickly moving to the top of the agenda for many of us.

The answer needn't be complicated. But like all things worth doing, becoming investment-savvy requires some study and some perseverance. I'm going to try to cut through the fog. I'm going to talk straight about why and how you should be thinking about your money and your future.

I'm not out to prove I'm smarter than you are or that I have all the answers. In fact, I know I don't have all the answers, and I may not be smarter. But I'm smart enough to know you shouldn't need a fancy financial vocabulary or a degree in finance to do some common-sense planning for your future.

My bias

Right up front, here's my bias: *I like facts.* I like proven principles, not just accepted wisdom or broad generalizations.

I agree with Oliver Wendell Holmes, who once said, "I never heard a generalization worth a damn, including this one." So I'm going to emphasize what is provable and scientific and show you the fallacy of so much of what is generally believed. I'm going to tell you, based on more than a quarter-century of helping people with their money, what really works and what doesn't. Further, I'm going to promulgate *Lucia's Laws*—many of which may be the direct opposite of the investment axioms you've heard for years. And with any kind of luck, you will not only learn some things but have a few grins along the way, too.

Why all the concern about retirement, anyway?

Americans are living longer, a lot longer. A century ago, life expectancy was 47.3 years. But now it's 76.5 years on average and in a few decades will be 82.6. Millions upon millions—quite possibly you among them—will live to be more than 100. (The future Willard Scotts will be very, very busy.) In fact, already the number of people 65 or older has grown by 56% since the 1970s. For the first time in history, there are more seniors than teenagers!

Meanwhile, workers are retiring earlier, voluntarily or otherwise. While your parents and grandparents may have died on the job or within a few years after retiring, many of your generation will live 20, 25, or 30 years after quitting work.

All this is good news for those of us in our middle- or later-years, right? Sure . . . *if* you plan for it.

But consider:

- There's enormous uncertainty about life spans. One study showed that even if you toss out extreme cases—where both spouses died quickly or lived to be very old—among those who remain, the second spouse to die might live to be 83 . . . or last to age 97. So . . . if you're in that big middle group, you may need to fund an 18-year retirement, *or* one that lasts 32 years. That's an enormous range.

- 70% of all couples 65 or older will have one or the other spouse in a nursing home. That's almost ¾ of senior couples. The average stay in a nursing home is 2.7 years at approximately $44,000 a year, or about $119,000, almost all of which isn't covered by Medicare. And the costs are accelerating at a rate that far exceeds inflation.

- Yet the median savings among adults in their late 50s—just the age when we start thinking seriously about retirement—are less than $10,000.

Even if you're lucky enough to stay out of a nursing home and avoid a big non-reimbursable medical expense, living longer is likely to erode your resources as inflation eats up more and more of your savings. While you may plan to leave money to your kids or favorite charity, you might end up needing every penny saved—and then some.

I'm not trying to scare you with these statistics. But I am trying to make you aware that the realities of retirement are that—unless you plan ahead and act on those plans—you can very easily run out of money before you run out of years. And that's not so good. It's not good for you, for your children, for your society.

And what's more, it's in many cases a preventable problem. That's what this book is all about: Helping you become self-sufficient in retirement. Which leads us to . . .

Lucia's Law   1

The government isn't going to take care of you.

I'm sorry. I wish it were otherwise. But even if its much-discussed problem of too many beneficiaries being supported by too few workers is fixed, Social Security just isn't going to be enough. Social Security was intended to be a financial side dish, not the main course. Don't assume you're going to be pleased with what's on your plate if Uncle Sam is the only cook you're counting on.

Meanwhile, the number of active workers covered by company pensions is fast declining. The reasons are numerous. Employees now are less likely to stay at one firm for a long time. Pension plans are costly to run. Pensions at some firms have taken a back seat to stock options and other benefits. Thus . . .

Lucia's Law | 2

Don't count on your employer to take care of you, either.

Company pensions are being dismantled in favor of plans like the 401(k), the 403(b), Simple IRAs and others that shift the burden of saving and investing from employers to employees. These plans can be confusing. But they also give the retiree lots of opportunities.

So the bad news is that it's up to you to make plans. But the good news is: For most people, that's do-able. With a bit of smarts and some time, we ought to be able to do this. And we *can.*

The twin demons— inflation and taxes

In addition to greater longevity, inflation and taxes are two other factors to keep in mind as you begin to think about your retirement nest egg. You're probably old enough to remember the late '70s and early '80s—leisure suits, *Mork and Mindy,* and double-digit inflation. Rates on CDs (certificates of deposit) got up to 15% or more. A great time to be an investor, right?

Wrong. Returns after taxes and inflation often were in negative territory, meaning that though you received higher interest payments, your purchasing power—your "real" rate of return—actually declined. (Figuring your real rate of return is easy. Take the yield on your fixed investment, subtract the percentage you'll pay in taxes, then subtract the rate of inflation.)

When interest rates were 15%, inflation was also in the double digits. And the real rate of return on fixed investments was under water.

Compared to then, inflation right now is relatively tame. But, still, inflation is ever-present and over time will rob you. Even with inflation at 3%, the purchasing power of a dollar is cut in half in a little more than 23 years. That means in two decades you'll need twice as much money to buy what you do now.

Similarly, taxes can take away so much of what you make. So we need to think about tax-managing our money. One example I often use in my seminars illustrates the effect of such taxes, or lack of. Let's say Christopher Columbus, when he sailed across the ocean blue in 1492, put $1 in a savings and loan and let it earn interest. What do you think that'd be worth today?

Well, 500 years is a long time (longer than *my* investment horizon). But at simple interest, Chris would now have amassed only $26—that's $25 in simple interest, plus his original investment of one buck. Aha, you say, what if the interest were compounded? If the interest was compounded but earnings were taxed annually, Columbus would now have $6.9 million. Interest on interest is a *beautiful* thing!

But here's the kicker: If the interest was compounded but the taxes were deferred, the good captain would now have $39 billion, with a "B." So you see just how important compounding in a tax-controlled environment can be. Keep that in mind. We'll come back to that.

And your point is . . . ?

My point is that in any investment strategy you choose, you not only want to make your money grow, you also need to take inflation and taxes into account. Which leads to . . .

Lucia's Law   3

It's not what you make . . .
but what you keep that counts.

It's that "real" rate of return that will be so important. By real rate, I mean your after-tax, after-inflation rate of return.

What you've heard about stocks is true, sort of

For years now you've probably heard that the stock market is the place to be. Its growth averages more than 10%

a year. Can any CD or money-market fund match that? No, they can't. With savings accounts paying 2% or 3%, stocks look pretty good. Yes, indeed.

Further, you've doubtless heard that some people—maybe those you know at work or on the golf course—hit it big with Qualcomm, AmericaOnline, or Something-orother.dotcom—and made an incredible bundle. Possible? Yes.

In fact, I believe I can safely say . . .

Lucia's Law | 4

If you don't invest in stocks . . .
you won't be financially prepared for retirement.

Chart 1-1 shows the return from stocks, bonds, and cash before and after inflation. Stocks, as you can see, have a decided edge in terms of real return. So if that's the case, why not just put your money in the stock market, then sit back in your chaise lounge and reflect on your soon-to-be luxury yacht and million-dollar villa? Well, it's not that simple. And Chart 1-2 shows why.

Chart 1-2 is my EKG. No, just joking! Actually Chart 1-2 shows the *wide* fluctuations in the S&P500 index over the years. (. . . but my EKG probably does look like that during periods of market turbulence.) The stock market is a real roller coaster because, for starters, there are 20,000-some

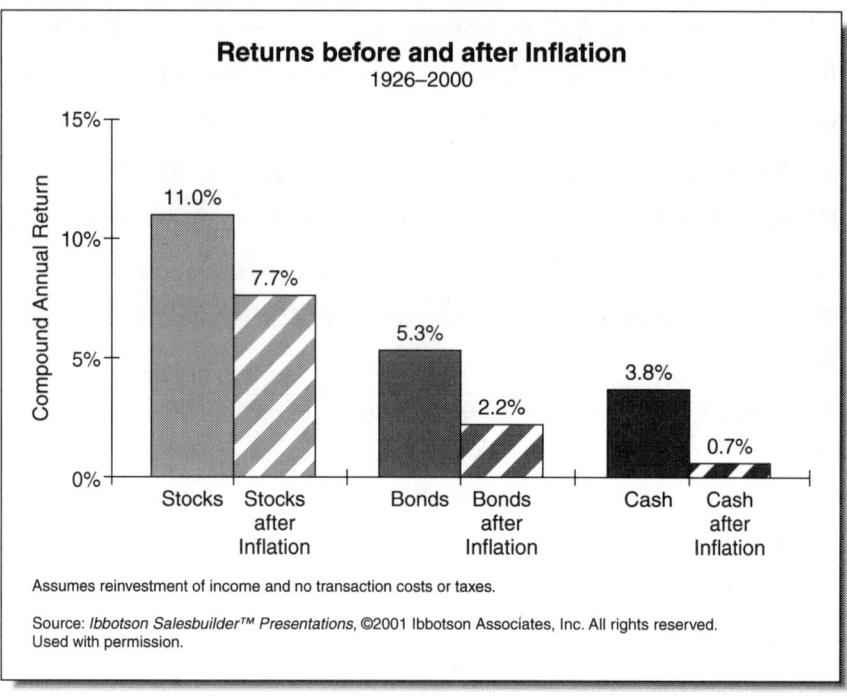

Chart 1-1

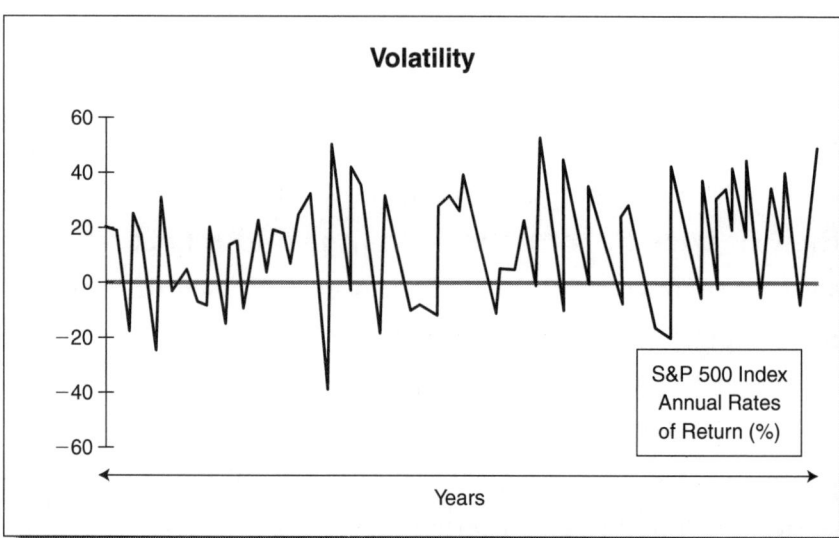

Chart 1-2

stocks, and they're not all winners—and even the winners don't win year in, year out. And the overall market doesn't perform consistently. That 10%+ average growth figure you've heard about is just that—an *average*. It may be up 30% one year and down 20% the next. (Be wary of averages. The average American family, for example, consists of 2.6 persons—but how many have you seen like that?)

No doubt about it, stocks are risky—at least in the short-term. In fact, stock brokers and mutual fund managers are so fond of one phrase that they put it in almost all their literature: "Past performance is not necessarily an indicator of future results." That means, "We don't have any idea what's going to happen." And it's true, they don't. *No one* does.

So that unpredictability is a problem for those who are trying to plan for retirement. Because what do you want when you retire? You want to be able to count on a certain level of income, right? Sure. You also want that income to grow to cover inflation.

So if stocks and the equity market is the place to be, but stock prices bounce every which way, how are you going to get that kind of certainty? Good question. I'm glad you asked that. Because that's what this book is all about.

But before we get into the details of the *Buckets of Money*® principle, let's look at why the usual methods of investing in the stock market don't work. You may recognize some of these money-making methods, maybe even some that you're so fond of that you use them yourself. But keep an open mind. And I predict that as you see the shortcomings of these other efforts, the logic of *Buckets of Money*® will become clear.

Ideas That Sound Good . . . But Aren't Good and Sound

❑ **Time the Market**

O.K., the market jumps around a lot. We all know this. So what do we do? Well, if we can anticipate those jumps, sell just before it goes down and buy just before it goes up, we'll be golden, right? Yes, we would. Golden, indeed.

But here's the rub: *Nobody is smart enough to do that.* The market is affected by all sorts of factors, here and abroad: interest rates, government policies, consumer confidence, bad news, good news, currency fluctuations, the ups and downs of earnings, even the health of heads of state. Not me, not you, not Warren Buffett, not Bill Gates, not Peter Lynch knows what's going to happen tomorrow or even five years from tomorrow.

In fact, speaking of Lynch, I once interviewed him. I asked this fabled money manager at Fidelity Investments what he thought was ahead for the stock market. "We'll see," he said. I asked him the same question about the bond market. "We'll see," he repeated. I asked him about interest rates, and he said. "If I could predict the direction

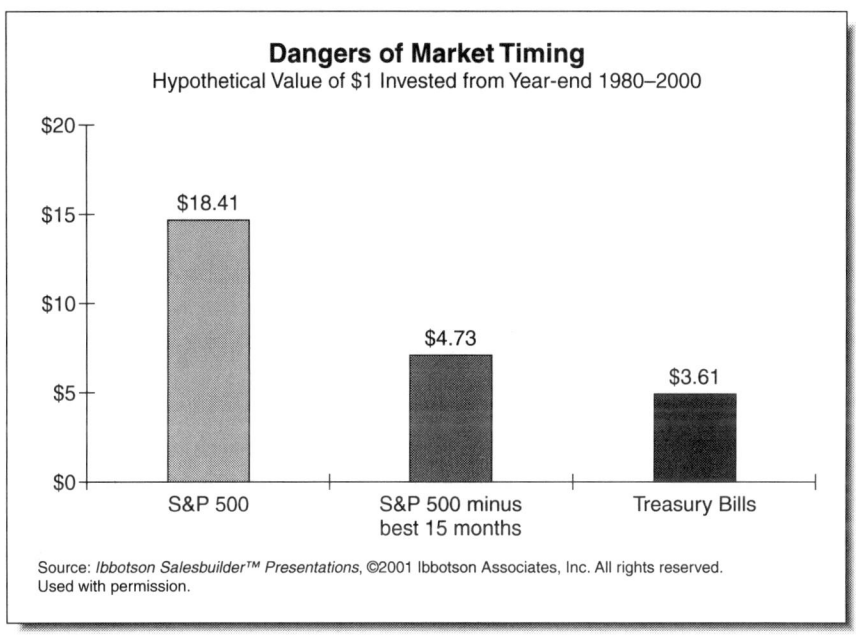

Dangers of Market Timing
Hypothetical Value of $1 Invested from Year-end 1980–2000

Source: *Ibbotson Salesbuilder™ Presentations*, ©2001 Ibbotson Associates, Inc. All rights reserved.
Used with permission.

Chart 1-3

of interest rates three times in a row, I'd be a billionaire."
This was Peter Lynch, the most successful and admired
money manager of his generation and one of my heroes,
and he doesn't know. If *he* doesn't, neither do you or I.

In about 20 of the last 70 calendar years, stocks have
lost money. In truth, when the market makes big gains, it
often does so in leaps within a few days' time. So if you're
not fully invested, it's easy to miss a major move.

In short, you can't predict a good day. As Chart 1-3
shows, $1 invested in the Standard & Poors 500 for 20
years (1980–2000) would have grown to $18.41. But miss
just the 15 best months (out of 240) in that 20 years, and
you'd end up with only $4.73.

Moral: *It's better to stay invested in some good stocks or good funds.* But most people don't. They get impatient. They see that some other fund or stock is going gangbusters, and they can't help but chase the front-runners. They get a hold of that 1-800-SWITCHMYFUND number and use it all the time to jump on this fund or drop that one—and end up shooting their portfolio in the foot. As you probably have figured out by now, I'm not the biggest fan of market timing.

That's because it *can't* be done. Stock prices move—up or down—so rapidly and sometimes so utterly without warning than even if you were able to get out of the market before it took a tumble, you wouldn't know when to get back in. Thus, you'd likely end up worse off than if you'd never gotten out.

Which is exactly what happens to market timers and which bring us to . . .

Lucia's Law | 5

Too much trading can be hazardous to your wealth.

As I say, you can't predict a good day. And if you pick a bad day to get in or out of the market, you may be paying for it for a long time. Chart 1-4 shows the results of a five-year study in which the more investors traded, the less well they did.

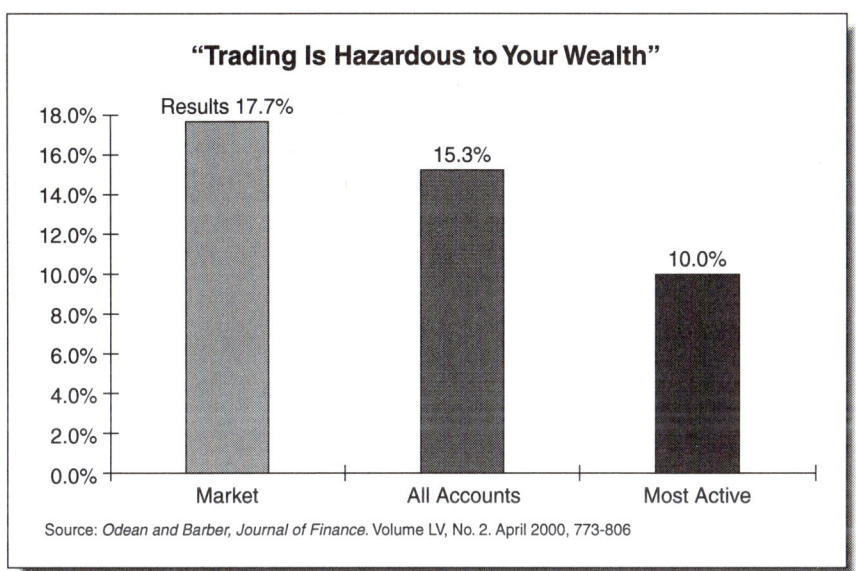

Chart 1-4

❏ Follow the Leader

Another tactic that leads investors astray is following the latest financial Pied Piper. Millions of people scan the ratings of mutual fund managers, for example, to find those whose funds performed best the previous year. But rarely is "Past Performance Is Not Necessarily an Indicator of Future Results" more true than here.

After all, whom would you choose: the manager who made the most money in the 1987 crash? Or, the one who lost more than average in '87? Well, according to the *Hulbert Financial Digest*, in the five years following the '87 crash, the managers who did best in the crash made 1.4% while the crash losers earned an average of 5.1%. (Why are we even buying all these magazines that purport to tell us who the best fund managers are?

Beats me. Maybe we should be looking for lists of the *worst* managers!)

In fact, *Hulbert* reports, for the decade ending in 1992, if you jumped each year to the best fund manager of the past 12 months, you'd have gained 51.2% over 10 years. But if you had begun each year investing with the *worst* manager of the previous 12 months, your account would have gone up 220% over the same period! And . . . even so, both would have earned less than the S&P 500 Index, which climbed 308% during that time.

Thus, I conclude . . .

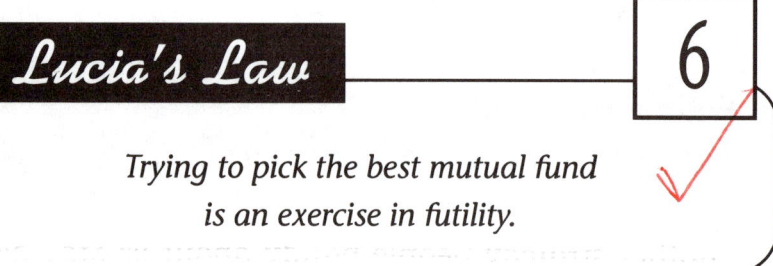

Lucia's Law

6

Trying to pick the best mutual fund is an exercise in futility.

A whole financial-magazine industry has sprouted around the idea of trying to get you into the hottest of the 10,000-some mutual funds. But here's the reality: If you pick a manager or a fund that finished in the bottom fourth of all funds, you have a 50% chance of finishing above the median five years later. And if you pick a top-quartile manager or fund, you have a 48% chance of finishing above that same median. So, in short, whether you pick the top fund or the worst, your chances of doing well over time are about the same.

The predictive abilities of the magazines and newsletters don't amount to much over the long term. Even the much-vaunted Morningstar ratings service, while great for the information it provides, isn't terrific at predicting future winners. All fund ratings are based on what happened yesterday, but no one knows what will happen tomorrow. My advice: Pick what seems to be a mix of good but diverse funds and stick with them.

As for those self-proclaimed investment gurus who flood you with junk-mail or claim on TV to have a lock on future riches, well, they're doing little more than reading tea leaves. Ask yourself: If their strategy is *so* great, wouldn't they be so really, really rich that they wouldn't need to appear on infomercials selling some get-rich-quick scheme? You bet.

❑ Be American, Buy Only American

Another strategy people bandy about is: Stay away from foreign stocks. Overseas companies are less safe, these investors say. I say: Nuts to that.

Yes, our economy has often done well in recent decades. But don't make the mistake that the international markets have nothing to offer. Chart 1-5 shows that while the American stock market did well over the past 30 years, it wasn't the best-performing.

Two decades ago, as author Ric Edelman points outs, America accounted for almost 50% of the world's total stock-market capitalization. Today, it represents 43%. Does that mean we're in decline? Actually, it just means that

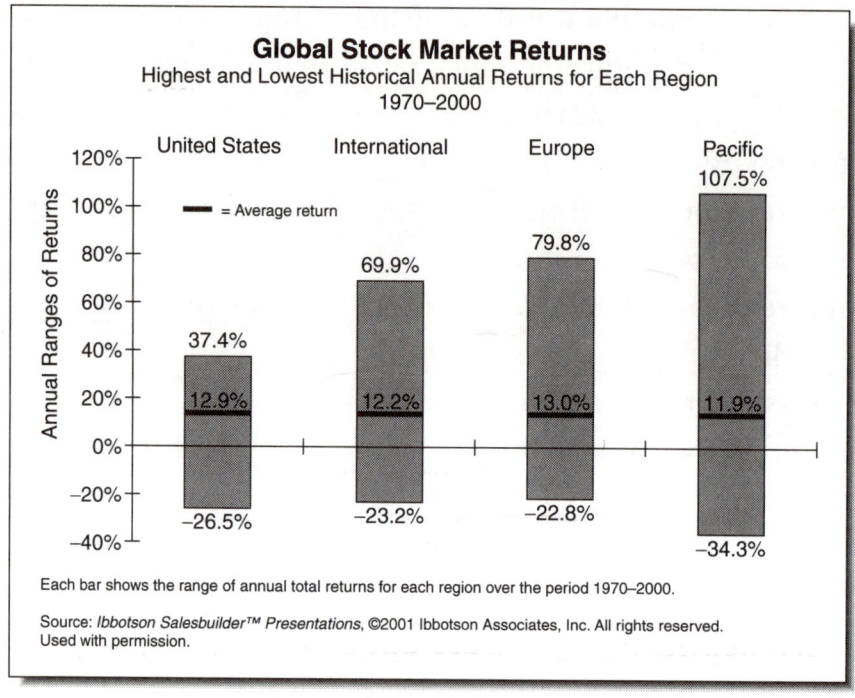

Chart 1-5

we're a smaller piece of a very rapidly-growing pie. And that's why you need to have at least some of your money in international stocks.

While I usually recommend an allocation of 20%, Chart 1-6 shows how you can put as much as 40% of your portfolio in foreign equities and have no more risk—and a *much* higher potential return—than if you were totally invested in U.S. stocks. Thus, if you don't invest overseas, you may miss out on the often-stellar performance of international stocks.

❑ **Stick with One Investing Style**
Others advocate using just one style of investing. Value investors, for example, look for bargain stocks that have

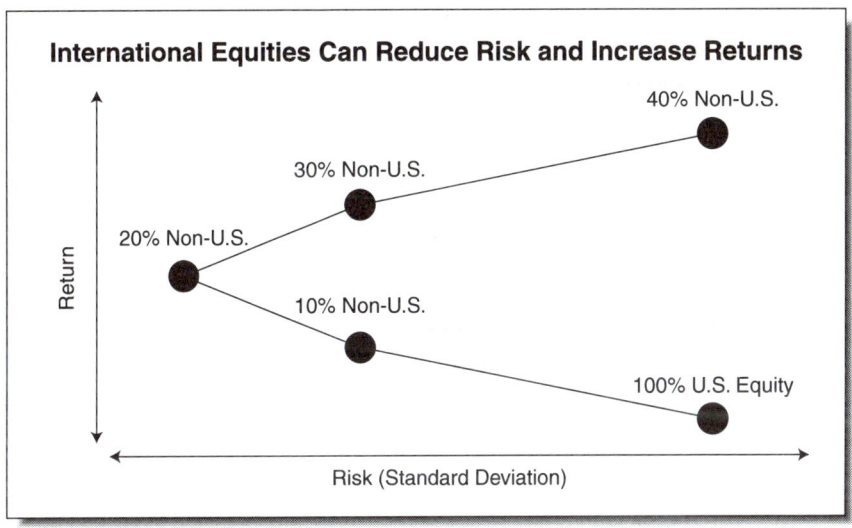

Chart 1-6

been beaten down and are due for a rise; they buy low in hopes of later selling high. Growth investors, on the other hand, like more expensive, high-flying companies; they buy high in hopes of selling even higher. Yet others prefer to concentrate on certain sectors, such as only large companies, or only small companies, or just those in the energy field or the retail field or the electronics field . . . or *some*thing. But none of those schemes work consistently.

And just because you're invested in a mutual fund rather than an individual stock doesn't mean you're diversified. Some stock funds are so specialized that they are almost as risky as owning a single firm's stock. (What's more, even a stock fund's name can be misleading. The manager of a large growth fund may load up on small-capitalization stocks when they're hot. It pays to read the prospectus and annual report.)

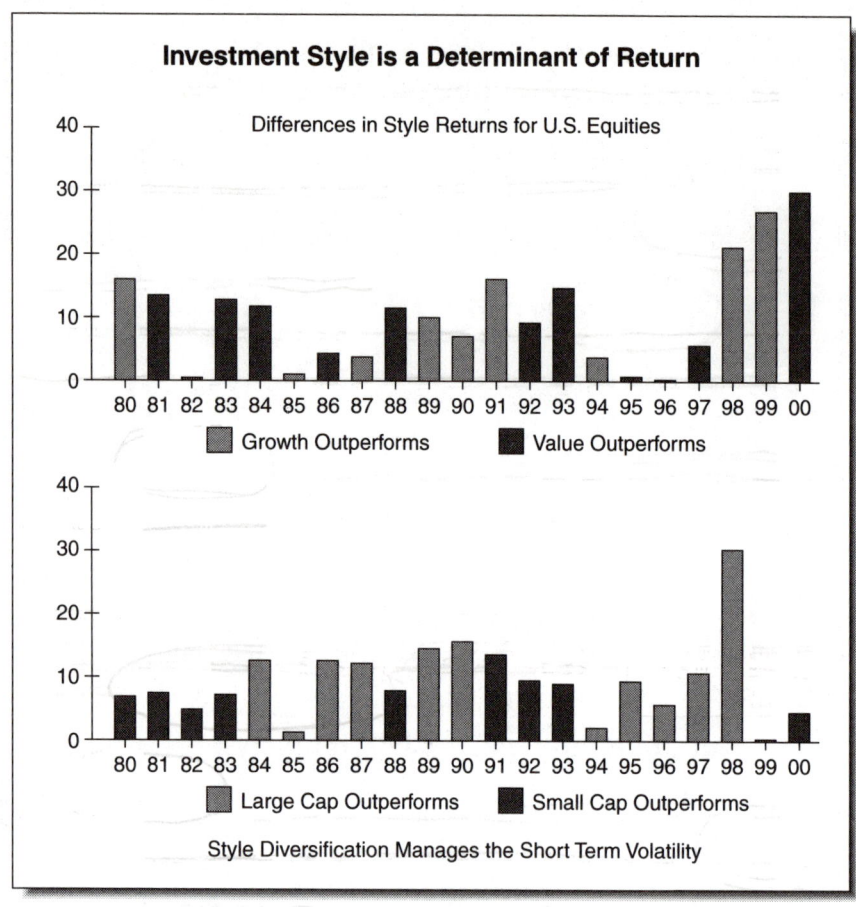

Chart 1-7

The truth is, all styles of investing are cyclical and fraught with peril. Chart 1-7 for example, shows how the results of investing by styles defy predictability. And Chart 1-8 illustrates how the return of different investment classes varies markedly from year to year.

The moral of the story

Just as we've seen all along, nobody is smart enough to know what's going to be in favor or out of favor in five

Relative Performance of Market Sectors

Rank	1985	1986	1987	1988	1989	1990	1991	1992	1993	1994	1995	1996	1997	1998	1999	2000
1	FOREIGN STOCK	FOREIGN STOCK	FOREIGN STOCK	SMALL CAP Value	LARGE CAP Growth	BONDS	SMALL CAP Growth	SMALL CAP Value	FOREIGN STOCK	FOREIGN STOCK	LARGE CAP Growth	LARGE CAP Growth	LARGE CAP Growth	LARGE CAP Growth	SMALL CAP Growth	SMALL CAP Value
2	LARGE CAP Growth	LARGE CAP VALUE	LARGE CAP Growth	FOREIGN STOCK	LARGE CAP VALUE	LARGE CAP Growth	SMALL CAP Value	LARGE CAP VALUE	SMALL CAP Value	LARGE CAP Growth	LARGE CAP VALUE	LARGE CAP VALUE	SMALL CAP Value	FOREIGN STOCK	LARGE CAP Growth	BONDS
3	SMALL CAP Value	BONDS	LARGE CAP VALUE	LARGE CAP VALUE	SMALL CAP Growth	LARGE CAP VALUE	LARGE CAP Growth	SMALL CAP Growth	LARGE CAP VALUE	LARGE CAP VALUE	SMALL CAP Growth	SMALL CAP Value	LARGE CAP VALUE	LARGE CAP VALUE	FOREIGN STOCK	LARGE CAP VALUE
4	SMALL CAP Growth	LARGE CAP Growth	BONDS	SMALL CAP Growth	BONDS	SMALL CAP Growth	LARGE CAP VALUE	BONDS	SMALL CAP Growth	SMALL CAP Value	SMALL CAP Value	SMALL CAP Growth	SMALL CAP Growth	BONDS	LARGE CAP VALUE	SMALL CAP Growth
5	LARGE CAP VALUE	SMALL CAP Value	SMALL CAP Value	LARGE CAP Growth	SMALL CAP Value	SMALL CAP Value	BONDS	LARGE CAP Growth	LARGE CAP Growth	SMALL CAP Growth	BONDS	FOREIGN STOCK	BONDS	SMALL CAP Growth	BONDS	FOREIGN STOCK
6	BONDS	SMALL CAP Growth	SMALL CAP Growth	BONDS	FOREIGN STOCK	FOREIGN STOCK	FOREIGN STOCK	FOREIGN STOCK	BONDS	BONDS	FOREIGN STOCK	BONDS	FOREIGN STOCK	SMALL CAP Value	SMALL CAP Value	LARGE CAP Growth

Chart 1-8

years or so. Still, folks make wrong, short-term decisions all the time and for the wrong reasons. They buy high when a stock or mutual fund is said to be "hot." And then they sell in a panic when, inevitably, it dips.

One of my favorite financial authors is Ric Edelman (*The Truth About Money*), who puts it so succinctly: "Stocks are not the problem—you are the problem, because you let your emotions get in the way."

Edelman and I and every other capable financial planner say you must invest in stocks if you're going to keep ahead of inflation. But by now you're probably asking: "If, as you say, I need to be in the market but I can't begin to time its ups and downs . . . and can't consistently pick the best stocks or funds . . . and can't count on the best managers . . . and can't rely on a certain style of investing, how can I financially prepare for retirement?"

The answer: Buy quality, well-diversified investments, then have a plan that gives you the means as well as the discipline and/or courage to hold them for years. That's also—*surprise!*—the gist of the *Buckets of Money*® principle. But before we jump right into the Buckets, let's look more closely at the important question of what we mean by "diversified."

Chapter 2

WHY YOUR GRANDMOTHER WAS RIGHT AFTER ALL!

A lot of folks, perhaps you among them, hate the idea of financial risk. To these investors, the wild plunges and peaks of the stock market seem to epitomize such risk-taking. They feel they worked hard for that money, they and/or their kids are going to need it, and by gosh, they don't want to fritter it away by investing it in something that's as likely to go down as it is up.

That's understandable. But it's also short-sighted and self-defeating.

Every investment involves risk. Truth is, even *not* investing involves risk. (Hoarding cash under your mattress may give you a sense of security but it doesn't protect you if the house burns down . . . or much more likely, if inflation devours the purchasing power of those greenbacks.) So understand . . .

Lucia's Law

7

There's nothing wrong with putting your money at risk.
In fact, it's impossible not to.

So the real question *isn't:* Shall I risk my money? You will, no matter what you do. The real questions are: *How* shall I risk my money? *How* can I get some measure of protection while taking a small, calculated risk? In short, though every investment includes risks, wisdom consists of knowing what the risks are and which ones are worth taking.

Let me give you an example that financial planners sometimes use of how risk can help you. Let's say you have $50,000 to invest for 20 years. If you chose a 6% CD, your account would grow (before taxes) to $110,000. You would have risked little, except for the effect of two decades' worth of inflation.

But just for the sake of argument, imagine instead that you divided your $50,000 evenly as follows:

- $10,000 in an old coffee can buried in your backyard. At the end of the two decades, you'd still have a soggy $10,000 in an old coffee can.
- $10,000 as an interest-free loan to your less-than-reliable Uncle Charley. As you feared, he fails to pay

you back, so at the end of the 20 years, you'd have zip, zero, nothing from him.

- $10,000 in a bank account earning 2.5% interest, giving you $15,000 at the end of the period; and
- $10,000 in a Treasury bond earning 7.5%. In 20 years, you'd have $25,500.
- $10,000 in the stock market where it earns the historical average of 11% over the 20 years, amounting to $80,622.

So, you earned nothing on the first chunk. You essentially threw away the second amount by giving it to your deadbeat uncle. You got minimal returns on the low-risk bank account and an O.K. return on the super-safe government bonds. Only that last $10,000 had much upside potential.

Yet, adding this all up, your total return is $146,622— far more than you would have earned by stashing the whole amount in the ultra-safe CD.

How can that be? How could you throw away 10 grand, earn nothing on another $10,000, and next-to-nothing on a third increment, and still far outpace the CD returns? Because you took *a little more risk.* Not a lot more—remember: Just one-fifth of your savings went into stocks. But that was enough to boost your returns handsomely.

Also keep in mind that you can't lose more than the amount you invest. Thus, the $10,000 that you effectively threw away is still $10,000. But the amount you can make with a stock investment is, in return for some risk, potentially unlimited.

The trick, then, is to diversify your investments in such a way as to minimize your chances of losing everything and maximizing your shot at some big bucks. Or as my sainted Italian grandmother used to say, *"Nontchu putta alla u eggsa inna wona basaket,"* which translated means "Don't put all your eggs in one basket." Granny, though a little lacking in the details, had the right idea.

You don't want to take foolish risks; you don't want to be rash. But you need to be willing to take *some* risks to have any hope of a decent return. If you're one of those people who try to insulate themselves from risk by sticking only with low-risk, low-return investments, you're guaranteeing failure.

Or to put it another way . . .

Lucia's Law   **8**

The biggest risk may be taking too little risk.

What is risk?

Keener minds than mine have long struggled with how to quantify risk. The best gauge they have come up with is something called standard deviation. I don't want to get too technical here about how it's figured. What's important at this point is only that you know what it means. So consider this: An investment's rate of return bounces around—or "deviates"—each year. If it bounced around the same amount each year, this deviation would become "standard."

But, of course, it doesn't. So deviation measures the amount of annual fluctuation (and thus, the risk) that an investment can be expected to have. The higher the standard deviation, the greater the expected fluctuation and the greater the risk.

An investor who knows the standard deviation is much better armed than if he merely knows the average return (because an investment's return is almost always higher or lower than its average.) So when I talk about risk or when you see charts in this book that compare risks, the yardstick that's being used is standard deviation. Again, the higher the standard deviation, the greater the volatility and the greater the risk.

For example, Chart 2-1 shows the return and risk of three different portfolios. The one at the bottom (35% government bonds, 50% stocks, and 15% cash) has no more risk than the 100% government-bond portfolio but has a far better return. Naturally, you want low risk and high return, so that's the superior portfolio of the three.

We can experiment with different combinations to come up with different degrees of risk/return. Chart 2-2, for example, shows the risk vs. return of several kinds of investments over a long period. Notice that the Treasury

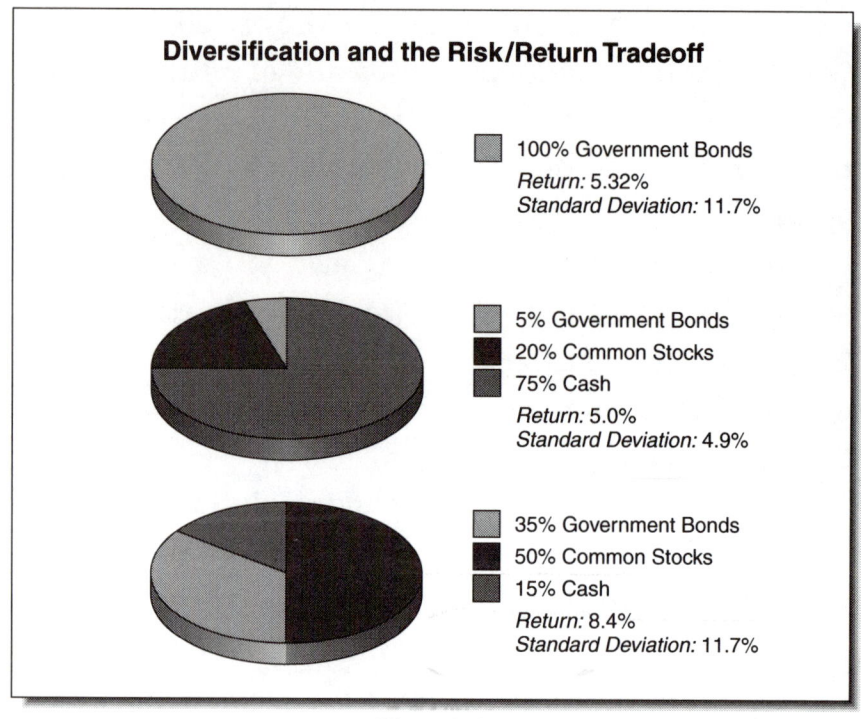

Chart 2-1

bills are low-risk, low-return. But as you move to the right (toward more risk), the returns start going up. It's that diversification—not just putting your money in one kind of investment—that gives portfolios the best shot at optimal returns.

How do we achieve diversity? Through what's called asset allocation. Asset allocation, in brief, means that what's important is not which stocks you buy but what proportion of your assets you have in the stock market as opposed to other investment categories.

Or, to quote me again (I'm *so* articulate!) . . .

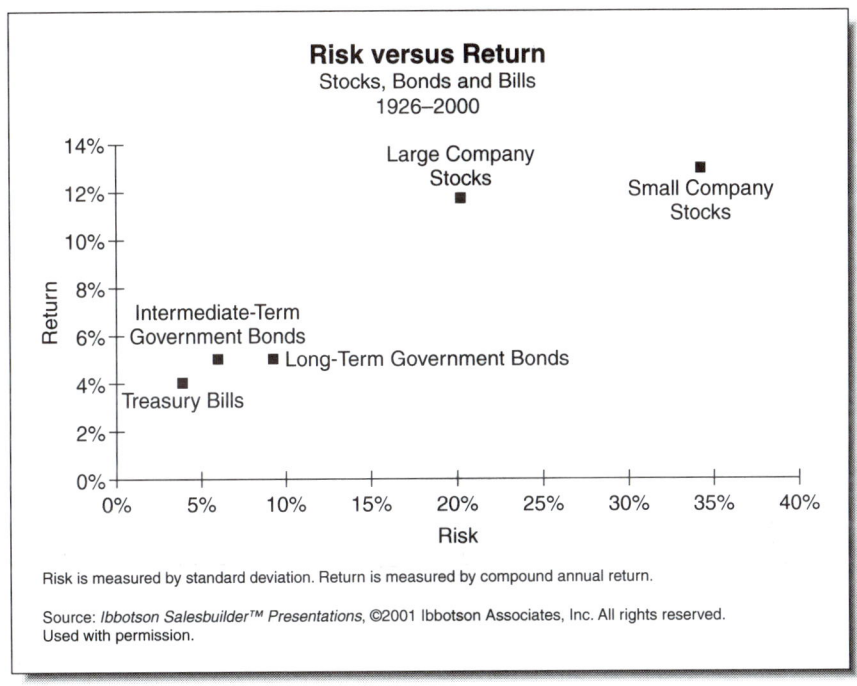

Chart 2-2

Lucia's Law ⟨9⟩

Forget about picking the next Home Depot or Fidelity Magellan. Instead . . . get the right asset mix.

But this isn't just my brilliant idea. It's based on research that led to the 1990 Nobel Prize in Economics. A very smart guy named Harry Markowitz came up with the foundation of diversification when he looked at what's the best way to make money in the stock market. (I enjoyed a delightful lunch with Mr. Markowitz one day, but I must admit to a strong case of "brain overload" as I attempted to keep up with his incredible mind. Afterward, I figuratively kicked myself for not studying harder in my college statistics courses.)

Not all risks are created equal

In effect, Markowitz developed techniques to help achieve the maximum likely overall return with the least possible risk. Such methods, called modern portfolio theory, are now routinely used by sophisticated investors and pension-plan trustees. The basic idea is that the total risk of a portfolio depends not just on the risks of an individual investment—but on the correlation between those risks.

As I've said before, all investments entail risk. But not all entail the *same* risk. Bond prices, for example, are very sensitive to interest-rate changes. Stocks are, too, but less so than bonds. CDs, fixed annuities, and guaranteed investment contracts fluctuate even less. Thus, in a period when interest rates are going up, you'd have less risk with a portfolio of bonds *and* stocks and CDs than you would with a 100% bond portfolio. Make sense?

So you can build a portfolio that's safer and more profitable by investing in many asset classes (*e.g.,* stocks, bonds, cash) than you can by investing in only one class. It might seem paradoxical, but introducing an element of stock-market risk (for example, going for a 20/80 stocks/ bonds mix instead of 100% bonds) can actually reduce the overall risk over time.

In fact, studies have shown that more than 90% of a portfolio's return is based on asset mix, not on what individual assets you choose or how well you time the market. To effectively diversify, you might divide your portfolio into numerous classes, say, large company stocks, small company stocks, international stocks, fixed-income, guaranteed investment contracts, and real estate.

Tailoring for your tolerance

You can—perhaps with help from a financial planner— further tailor these stocks/funds and other investments to match your risk tolerance. That means deciding between growth or value in the large- and small-cap stock sectors, between emerging and developed nations in the international sector, and between long- or short-term and high-credit or lower-credit ratings in the fixed-income sectors. Then regularly rotate your portfolio to keep the asset allocation balanced over time.

And though he hardly needs my ratification of his ideas, Markowitz was *right*. Such a portfolio provides better returns at a lower level of risk and volatility. Having a properly diverse portfolio means your returns probably will never be at the top of the pack. But they won't be at the bottom, either.

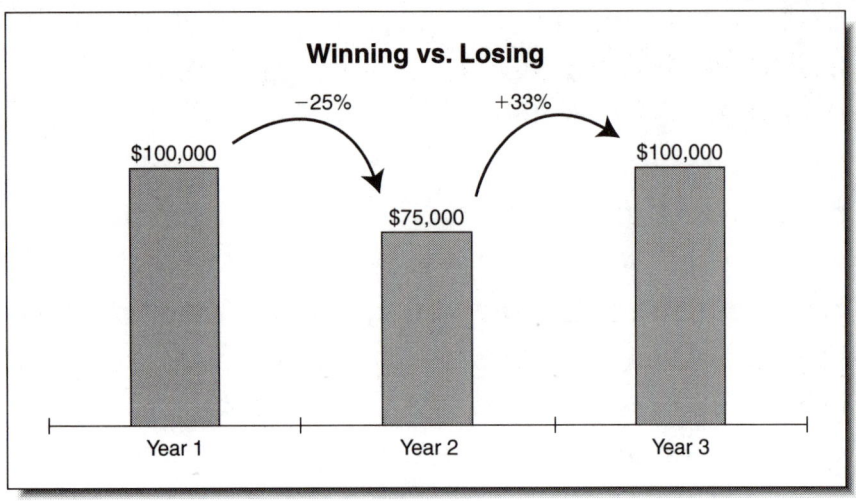

Chart 2-3

Why is that? Because most people don't have just one or two stocks; they own a bunch of stocks or funds, and their results aren't going to be too terribly different from the broad stock-market averages. If you owned just a few companies, you might wallop the averages—*or* get walloped. But as you add more stocks to your portfolio and add bonds and cash to your overall investment mix, you lower both your odds of greatly outpacing the market *or* of suffering a major beating if and when stocks head south.

And that's very important because once you've lost money, it's tougher to get back to where you were. For example, as Chart 2-3 shows, if your $100,000 nest-egg drops by 25%, you don't need a 25% but a *33%* gain to get you back to the original amount.

Investing to minimize loss must be part of any investment strategy. Thus, I humbly suggest . . .

Lucia's Law 10

The best way to win is to keep from losing.

It's like that example I talked about earlier in this chapter, the one where you threw away a sizeable chunk of your investment but still recouped by having a portion in stocks. You didn't earn as much as if you had put the whole $50,000 into stocks. But, still, you did well—and *without the risk* that you'd have faced if you had been totally invested in stocks and then there was a market collapse.

Diversification can help with your "real" rate of return, too. That's because not all investments are taxed the same or react similarly during inflation.

Bonds, for example, produce interest and stocks generate dividends. Both are taxed at your ordinary income-tax rate. But if you sell an investment for more than you bought it for, that's a capital gain. And if you have a net capital gain, the tax rate probably is going to be significantly less than what you'd pay on interest and dividends (and regular income).

Similarly, some asset classes (such as stocks and real estate) tend to do better in inflationary times than do fixed-income and cash investments. So, again, diversification—and a financial planner—can help you here. Charts 2-4 and 2-5 show the effect of taxes and inflation on different kinds of assets.

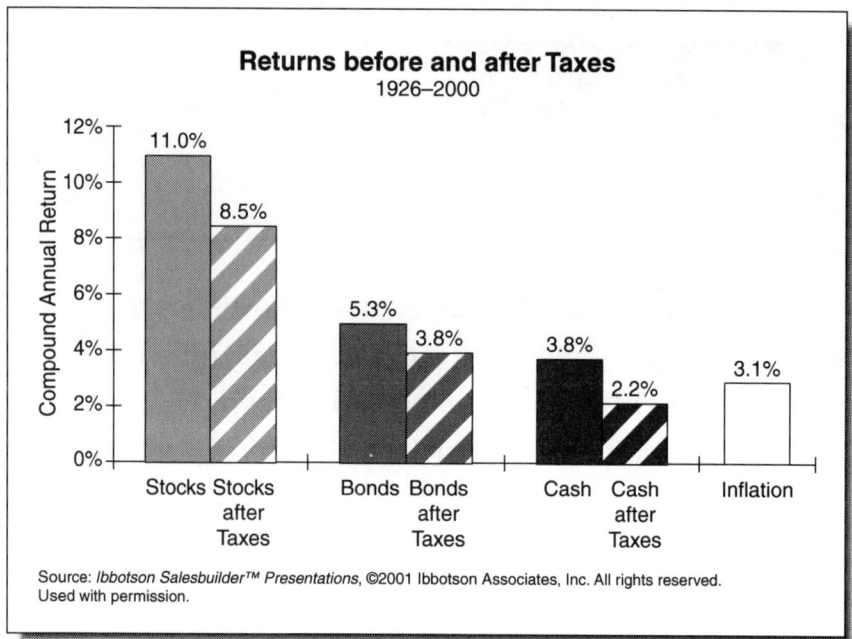

Chart 2-4

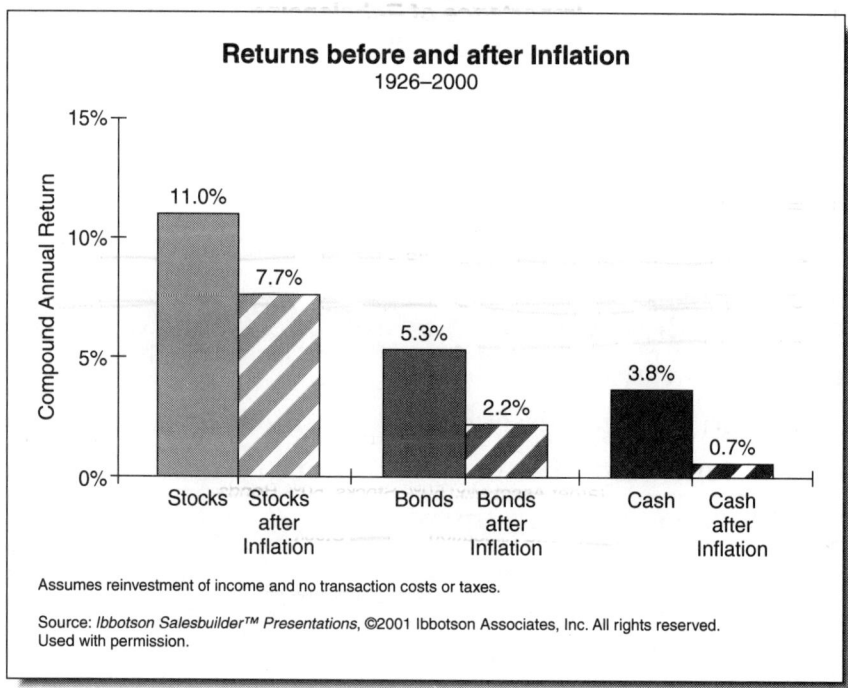

Chart 2-5

The joys of re-balancing

Notice that I said it's not enough just to diversify, you must also re-balance from time to time. That means setting targets for what percentages of your money should be in various assets (60% in stocks, say, and 20% in bonds, 20% in cash), then readjusting your portfolio from time to time to bring it back in line with these targets. Chart 2-6 shows, for example, how a stock/bond mixture can get out of whack because stocks generally grow more quickly than bonds, and Chart 2-7 shows how a portfolio might be tweaked to bring assets back into balance. If the portfolio isn't re-balanced, the stocks eventually would take

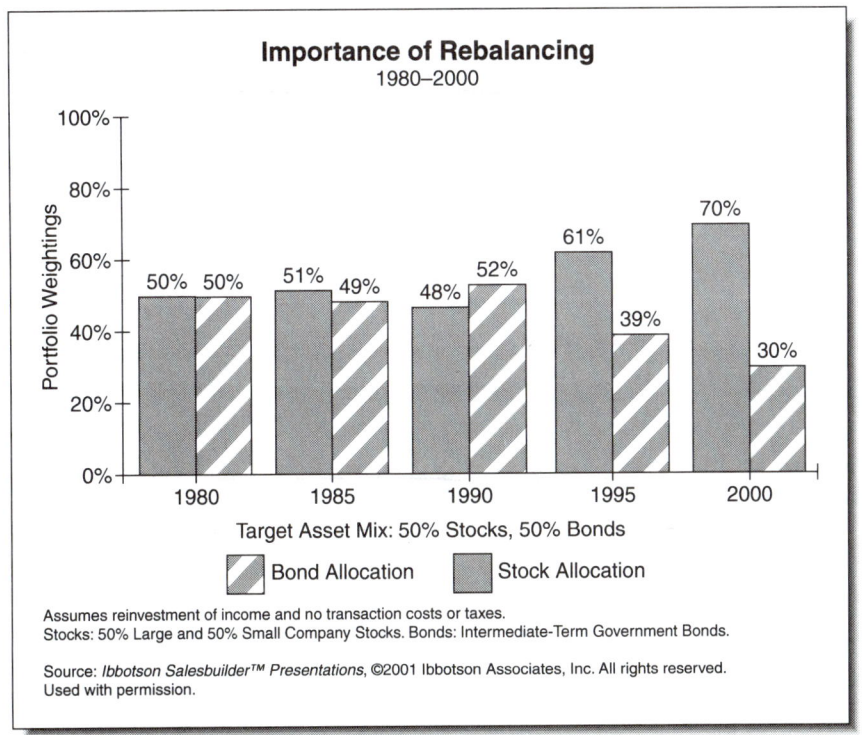

Importance of Rebalancing
1980–2000

Target Asset Mix: 50% Stocks, 50% Bonds

Bond Allocation   Stock Allocation

Assumes reinvestment of income and no transaction costs or taxes.
Stocks: 50% Large and 50% Small Company Stocks. Bonds: Intermediate-Term Government Bonds.

Source: *Ibbotson Salesbuilder™ Presentations*, ©2001 Ibbotson Associates, Inc. All rights reserved.
Used with permission.

Chart 2-6

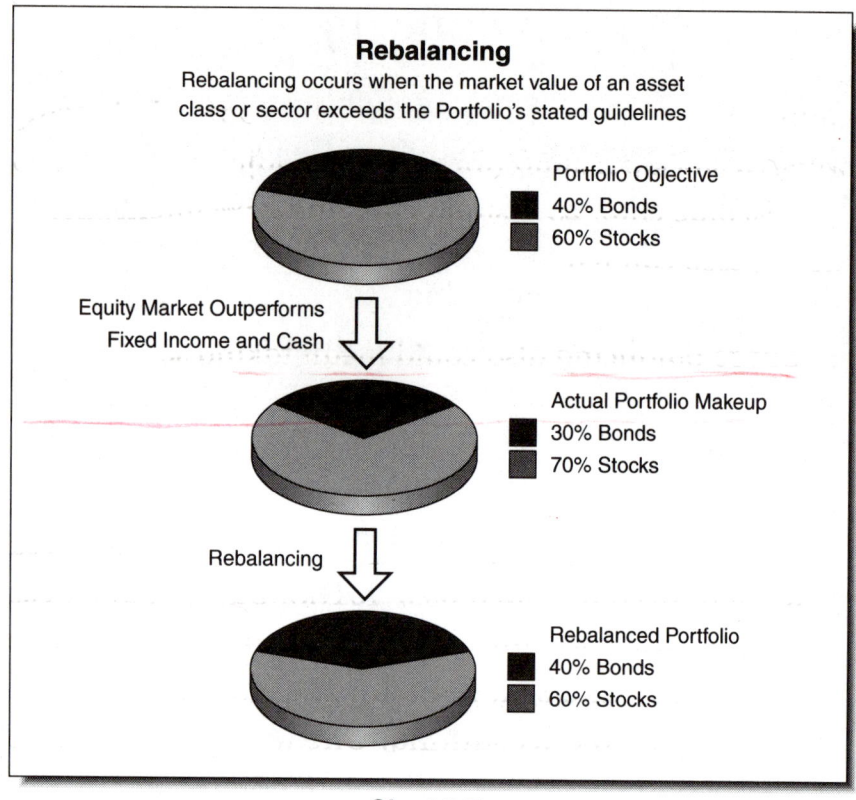

Rebalancing

Rebalancing occurs when the market value of an asset
class or sector exceeds the Portfolio's stated guidelines

Portfolio Objective
■ 40% Bonds
■ 60% Stocks

Equity Market Outperforms
Fixed Income and Cash

Actual Portfolio Makeup
■ 30% Bonds
■ 70% Stocks

Rebalancing

Rebalanced Portfolio
■ 40% Bonds
■ 60% Stocks

Chart 2-7

up more and more of your portfolio, increasing your exposure to risk if there was a steep stock-market downturn.

Your family may have taught you about this concept
of re-balancing. I know mine has. That's because when I
go to Las Vegas and get on a winning streak, my tendency
is to double down and bet the farm on a hot hand. My
wife Jeanne, bless her heart, has been known to scoop up
some chips when I'm not looking and stick them in her
purse. If I flame out, we still can go home with some winnings, thanks to her, because she has reduced our risk.

Re-balancing your portfolio is much the same. Re-balancing among stocks, bonds, and cash keeps your portfolio's risk level under control. In addition, re-balancing *within* a stock portfolio (for example: adjusting to a level of 50% blue chip, 25% small cap, and 25% international stocks) also can reduce risk if an over-weighted sector suffers a setback.

But re-balancing also could mean taking some dough out of other assets and putting it into stocks if they were beaten down to bargain prices. The point is, you re-adjust your stock portfolio to keep in sync with your goals.

This can be fairly simple and painless in a tax-deferred retirement account, such as a 401(k). But if your stocks are in a taxable account and/or if you pay commissions when you buy and sell, re-balancing can be costly and involve messy tax accounting. One way to avoid those problems is to direct new investment dollars to those investments that have become under-weighted. If stocks and bonds are outstripping your cash, for example, divert the money that you'd normally add to stocks/bonds into cash equivalents. Or you could take the dividends, interest, and mutual-fund distributions that are produced by your stocks and bonds and add them to your cash allocation.

To get your model back to its original proportions may seem to you like selling some of your winners and buying your losers . . . and that's what it *is*. But that may be a very good thing to do. If you don't re-balance, eventually you'll own almost all stocks and will have abandoned the concept of diversification.

It's not good to abandon diversification . . . just ask any tech-heavy investor who made a bundle in 1996–1999, but gave most of his winnings back in the "tech wreck" of 2000–2001. Re-balancing would have taken a few chips off the table, locking in at least some of those gains in companies like Cisco, Sun, Juniper, and JDS Uniphase before they tumbled.

Of course, you may not want to go back precisely to your original model. Your marital status, health, income, and other circumstances could have changed and, thus, your model may be altered.

How often should you reallocate or rebalance? Some people do it every couple years. Others do it when, for example, one asset class varies by some percentage from its initial weighting. I say: Whatever works for you is fine. In truth, *when* you do it is not as important as making a commitment *to doing* it.

So . . . just how risky is the market?

Ask me if the stock market is risky, and I'll ask you *how long* you expect to invest for. Chart 2-8 shows the reduction in risk over time in small- and large-company stocks, government bonds, and Treasury bills. Notice how the volatility shrinks with time. The longer you are invested in stocks, the less likely you are to have a loss (or for that matter, a phenomenal gain). Studies show that you've got about a 1-in-4 risk of losing money if you invest in stocks for one year.

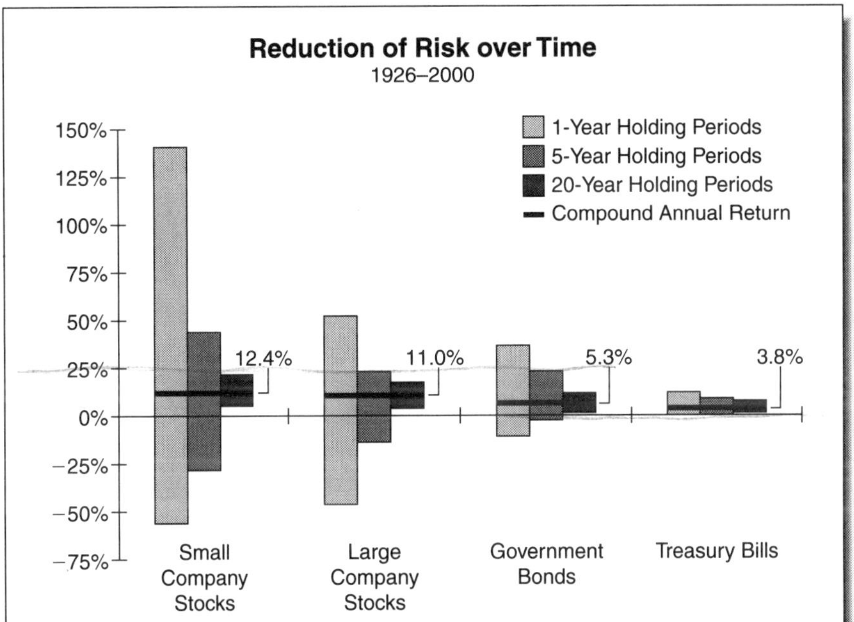

Reduction of Risk over Time
1926–2000

Legend:
- 1-Year Holding Periods
- 5-Year Holding Periods
- 20-Year Holding Periods
- Compound Annual Return

Small Company Stocks — 12.4%
Large Company Stocks — 11.0%
Government Bonds — 5.3%
Treasury Bills — 3.8%

Y-axis: 150%, 125%, 100%, 75%, 50%, 25%, 0%, −25%, −50%, −75%

Each bar shows the range of compound annual returns for each asset class over the period 1926–2000.

Source: *Ibbotson Salesbuilder™ Presentations*, © 2001 Ibbotson Associates, Inc. All rights reserved. Used with permission.

Chart 2-8

That's an important principle: Risk declines sharply the longer you remain in the market. And it's yet further evidence that you win by not losing. Please remember:

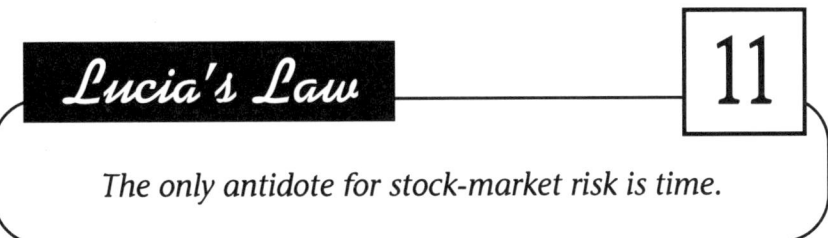

Lucia's Law | 11

The only antidote for stock-market risk is time.

And a corollary . . .

Lucia's Law **12**

If you have less than a 5-year time horizon in the stock market, you're a gambler, not an investor.

In a sense, investing in the stock market is primarily about time and only secondarily about money. When stocks fall, it's tempting to dwell on the money lost. But that loss doesn't really matter if you don't need to sell. In fact, if you're building up your retirement accounts, you'd probably prefer the market's gains to come later, after you've had a chance to build a big portfolio. A downturn now can actually be a plus for you because you'll be able to buy more shares with the same amount of money.

If you view your stocks from the perspective of time, you're more likely to make smart decisions and less likely to be unnerved when the market dives. If you're patient, well-diversified, and have a long-enough time horizon, you'll probably do O.K. But if you own just a few stocks or are heavily invested in a single sector, your wait could be awfully long for the market to spring back after a plunge.

Lessons learned?

I hope I've shown you that being totally risk-averse is, well, *risky*. And, further, I hope I've convinced you that:

- Though the stock market does fluctuate and often wildly so, you've got to have stocks over the long-term if you're going to meet your retirement goals;
- What stocks and mutual funds you choose is much less important than the proportion of your portfolio they occupy; and
- You've got to take a long-term view to allow the stock-market trend to work for you.

And that, my friends, is a guiding principle of the *Buckets of Money*® strategy: buying time to let the stocks and other long-term investments grow . . . while having enough income to live comfortably while that happens.

Chapter 3

WHAT KIND OF INVESTOR ARE YOU?

Meet the Nelsons, Ned and Nellie. Nice, hard-working folks, they are very proud of the fact that they have accumulated $300,000 in investable assets over their working years. The Nelsons want to enjoy their retirement, of course, and being conservative, they also want to make sure they don't lose any of that 300 grand. They toiled long and hard and did without in order to build that nest-egg, and they wouldn't feel comfortable risking their principal by investing in the stock market or making some other iffy investment.

What's more, they hope to leave most of that sum to their children and their grandchildren some day. So for the Nelsons, caution is the order of the day. Call them the Nervous Nelsons.

So what do they do? They keep the $300,000 in the bank, mostly in Certificates of Deposits. For them, it's perfect: The bank *guarantees* them an income on the money *with no risk to their principal.* And the deposit itself is insured by an agency of the government. What a deal!

At today's rates, the Nelsons will make about 6%—or $18,000 a year. That's not an enormous amount but the Nelsons are frugal, and with their Social Security added in, they'll get by. Equally important for them, they will sleep well at night. Because the government backs the CDs, they will still have their $300,000 no matter what. They've achieved, the Nelsons believe, safety *and* comfort.

But *have* they? No. *No,* in a very big way.

If inflation averages just 3% a year, the purchasing power of their yearly $18,000 in interest will almost be cut in half in two decades. That means buying the same amount of groceries, gasoline, and everything else will cost twice as much. It also means that as prices rise, the Nelsons will probably need to cash in some of their CDs just to get by. So their $300,000 is almost certain to shrink as they are forced into using more and more of it for everyday expenses.

Even if they somehow managed to keep the $300,000 intact, its *real* value—the amount it could purchase—will be closer to $150,000 than $300,000 after 20 years. And that's not at all what they had pictured and not what they intended to leave to their heirs.

Now the Nervous Nelsons really should be nervous. They chose such a conservative path that it's leading them to go broke. Or, as I like to put it . . .

Lucia's Law 13

Safety without performance equals . . . not much.

Above all, the Nelsons wanted their money to be safe. But they paid a big price for that illusion. They discovered a paradox: Focusing just on safety is a very *unsafe* way to invest. In fact, doing so practically ensures that you will fail financially.

CDs—sometimes called "Certificates of *Depreciation*" by financial wags—are not the basket you want to put all your eggs in. Yet they remain the investment of choice for many retirees like the Nelsons who prefer the apparent stability of CDs and the solidity that somehow attaches to something purchased from a bank.

Banks, particularly for a lot of seniors, have an aura of respectability. That image wins banks a lot of business. And that's fine. I'm in favor of respectability and in favor of banks—they do a good job at what they're designed to do, which is facilitate transactions. Banks are the perfect place in which to place your paycheck or Social Security benefit and then write checks on those accounts to pay your bills. They're also a good place to safely keep some cash while it's waiting for its ultimate destination.

But as a place to store your retirement cache, no way! As I like to put it . . .

> ## Lucia's Law   14
>
> *Leaving a lot of dollars in the bank is
> like leaving a bunch of hamburgers on the grill.
> They'll shrink right before your eyes.*

Banks as well as credit unions and savings and loans keep your money for you and pay you some interest to help keep abreast of inflation. But where's the *growth?* Not in banks, not in savings accounts or CDs. And you've got to get growth if you're going to build those retirement savings so they can support you through what may be a long retirement.

Safe from what?

Back to the Nelsons. They kept their money in a bank CD because it was supposed to be safe. But was it? And safe from *what?*

Well, it was safe in the very narrow sense that there is a government-sponsored insurance system designed to prevent a loss to depositors if the bank should default—that is, go out of business. (If default protection is your primary goal, though, investing in government securities would be even safer.) And it's safe in the sense that the Nelsons will get back their principal (but not the same purchasing power).

But while it's mildly reassuring that the bank probably won't go under and take the Nelsons' money with it, inflation and taxes pose much bigger risks to Ned and Nellie. And their CDs don't help them much there. Even if the inflation rate is a low 3%, that's half the interest rate of their CDs. So half of what they earn in interest is eaten up by inflation. Further, those interest payments are taxed at the Nelsons' regular-income rate. As a result, the Nelsons would probably be lucky to break even—and may even lose money from their "safe" investment.

In fact, the Nelsons' investment strategy is causing their savings to dwindle. They won't feel the loss immediately, but eventually they'll find their money is virtually all gone. Which may be a lot like having the dentist pull your tooth *slowly.*

Or take the Hendersons, Harry and Sherry. Harry read somewhere that the stock market has averaged something in excess of 10% per year returns since 1926. Harry, who considers himself shrewd, knew that CDs didn't pay anything like that. Neither did corporate bonds or Treasury securities.

So Harry and Sherry decided to go for it and invest all of their $300,000 in the stock market. They enjoyed doing the calculations: They should have $330,000 by the end of the first year, $363,000 by the second, $399,300 by the third year, and so on. In a little more than seven years, they figured, they would have doubled their money! They would have more than $600,000 in their retirement kitty—

and then let the party begin! Call them the High-Rolling Hendersons.

Unfortunately, for Harry and Sherry, they didn't read far enough, or maybe they chose to ignore the obvious. That 10% figure was an *average* gain, not one that occurred year in and year out. In fact, in some years, the stock market went down, *way down.* And some times way down for several years in a row.

In 1973 and 1974, for example, the market fell by almost 50%. And after that drop, it took years for an investment in the broad market to have earned enough to equal the guaranteed rates of CDs or Treasury bills.

If the High-Rolling Hendersons had retired and invested their $300,000 in a market like 1973–74, and then like the Nervous Nelsons, had taken out $18,000 each year to live on starting the year after a 50% decline, they would have been flat broke in just 17 years, even if the market averaged 10% annually for each year thereafter.

The Hendersons got greedy. By putting all their eggs in the stock-market basket, they were attempting to get rich quick. But by trying to do so they opened themselves up to enormous risk, proving the wisdom of what I'll now call . . .

Lucia's Law   **15**

*Try to get rich quickly—and you may get poor
even quicker.*

Yes, the stock market eventually came back from the 1973–74 debacle. But it would have been too late for the Hendersons. It turned out they had neither comfort nor safety.

So, you see, both the Nelsons and the Hendersons went broke. The risk-averse Nelsons went broke more slowly, but nonetheless just as broke because inflation ate away at what they thought was theirs forever. They were saddled onto a old horse called safety, and they rode him even as he collapsed and died on them.

By contrast, the Hendersons hitched themselves to what they thought was a shooting star that would arch endlessly across the financial sky. But we all know what happens to meteors—eventually, they crash or burn.

Using vastly different investment strategies, both the Nelsons and the Hendersons failed miserably at securing a safe, comfortable retirement. You can do better than they did, a lot better. To do so, you'll want to achieve a degree of safety (like the Nervous Nelsons) *and* you want growth (like the High-Rolling Hendersons). But not one of those to the exclusion of the other. Which leads to . . .

Lucia's Law   **16**

The goal of retirement planning isn't so much to get rich . . . as it is to avoid becoming poor.

How much safety and how much growth would work for your portfolio? Well, in part that depends on your personal makeup, your tolerance of risk.

Know thyself

Are you the sort of person who's intimidated by all the jargon and all the decisions that go with investing? Who looks at his portfolio as little as possible—maybe at tax-time and hardly at all the rest of the year? Who would sooner cut off an ear than buy anything "risky"? Who sleeps fitfully, if at all, when his 100 shares of Exxon drops a few points?

Or are you the kind who reads the *Wall Street Journal* for fun? Who knows the current prime rate to within an $\frac{1}{8}$ of a point? Who loves being asked, "What do *you* think is going to happen to the market?" Who thinks buying Internet stocks on margin is more fun than a picnic in the park?

Or, perhaps you're neither of the above. Maybe you're the type of investor who isn't as much frightened as he is just plain bored by the markets. Who finds studying his stocks about as exciting as watching grass grow? Maybe you think investing—like paper-training the puppy and cleaning the gutters—is O.K. as long as someone else does it. So you're inclined to delegate to anyone who shows the slightest hint that he knows what he's doing, even if that's your oft-unemployed brother-in-law.

Whatever your style, you may need to fine-tune it a bit as you head for retirement. This is a time to avoid being either foolhardy or overly cautious. And if you've used ignorance as an excuse not to get involved with your finances, perhaps retirement can be a helpful catalyst for change. Truth is, investing is not as complicated as some would make it. If you've got some patience and a willingness to learn a little, you can do well.

Lots of possibilities

Further, as we've already pointed out, Social Security and employer pensions probably aren't going to be enough to sustain you over a long retirement. In fact, some analysts say that for an average retiree, up to 60% of retirement income needs to come from his or her own investments. If so, you're going to need some investment skills, some information, and the right attitude. Ultimately, investing well comes down to having lots of information (possibilities), knowing the likelihood of something happening (risk), and having the mind-set to make the right decisions when they need to be made.

For many of us, risk evaluation is an emotional process. How you *feel* about risking your money—or conversely, how safe it must be—will affect many of your decisions as an investor. You could be ultra-conservative (like the Nelsons) who didn't want to risk one dollar or ultra-aggressive (like the Hendersons), who were ready to risk all or most of their money on the chance that it will grow wildly.

Most of us, fortunately, prefer a middle road. We want a mix of safe-but-slow investments as well as some higher-risk, higher-return possibilities.

A fit with your comfort level

Knowing something about your risk-tolerance may help you make decisions that'll give you both peace of mind and a feeling of accomplishment and success. Your strategy should not be too far out of line with your comfort level. Though your tolerance for risk may rise or fall depending on lots of factors—job security, confidence about the future, investment experience—over the long-run it's probably fairly consistent.

The conservative investor who goes against his instincts to invest heavily in penny stocks and commodities futures is probably going to feel uncomfortable no matter how well his portfolio fares. Similarly, an aggressive investor with all his money in savings bonds is going to be unhappy despite the so-called safety of that investment.

How much risk feels right to you?

The following, highly-unscientific quiz may give you an idea of your risk-comfort level. Some of the questions are finance-related, some are more about temperament.

Don't over-think your responses. There are no wrong answers. This shouldn't be stress-inducing, but rather just a quick read on whether you might need to nudge yourself toward being a bit more bold or rein yourself in if you tend to overreact when emotions run high.

Circle the answer that most closely approximates your likely action or opinion. There's a scoring guide at the end.

A. *On days when you hear on the news that the Dow Jones Average takes an enormous leap, do you:*
   1. Congratulate yourself on not being a part of that game?
   2. Pride yourself on having stocks for the long haul but plan to buy no more?
   3. Call your broker and try to get in while the getting is good?

B. *Your investing motto, if you had one, probably would be:*
   1. "A penny saved is a penny earned."
   2. "Patience is a virtue."
   3. "Go for it!"

C. *If you were in Las Vegas and in the mood for a game, you'd immediately head for:*
   1. Bingo
   2. The quarter slots
   3. Blackjack

D. *You're playing tennis. It's set-point, match-point, and your second serve. Do you:*
   1. Play it safe and hit an easy serve rather than double-fault?
   2. Hit a medium-hard serve, taking into account that you could lose the game—or win it—with this shot?
   3. Say to yourself "no guts, no glory," and try all-out for an ace?

E. *You're putting in an offer to buy a house you really want. You understand there's another interested buyer*

also composing an offer. The asking price is $299,999.
Do you:

1. Make an offer above the full price? "This one's not going to get away."
2. Offer full price? "What could be more fair than that?"
3. Offer $285,000? "The owners can lump it or leave it."

F. *You win $500 in a football pool at your health club.*
Do you:

1. Put it in an interest-bearing savings account?
2. Deposit it in your mutual-fund account?
3. Try to parley it into something bigger by buying a "hot" stock?

G. *You buy 200 shares of stock at $33. A week later, it soars to $45 on a strong profit report. Do you:*

1. Hold all 200 shares? "Why rock the boat?"
2. Sell 100 shares and look for another good, more reasonably-priced stock? "Nobody ever went broke taking a profit."
3. Buy more of the same on margin? "This baby's a winner."

H. *In a single week, you get three pre-approved applications for credit cards. Do you*

1. Toss them? "I don't need more plastic. In fact, I don't need *any* plastic."
2. Decide to look them over for a while, comparing annual fees and interest rates? "A smart decision might save me a few bucks."

3. Send 'em in? "A person can't be too rich, too thin, or have too much credit."

I. *You inherit $5,000 from a long-lost uncle. That's hardly enough to alter your lifestyle, so do you decide to:*
   1. Just put it in the bank and use it to help make your mortgage payments?
   2. Buy a bond or a bond fund?
   3. Buy a high-flying stock?

J. *The stock market turns south in a big way. So do you:*
   1. Sell?
   2. Decide to watch for a few months before deciding?
   3. Buy at bargain prices because a quick rebound is likely?

K. *Which of the following most closely describes your feelings toward investing:*
   1. Avoiding risk is more important than pursuing a high return.
   2. Preservation of principal is a high priority, but I'm comfortable with some risk to improve my return.
   3. I leap at above-average risk if it offers the hope of above-average returns.

L. *The way I feel generally about the future of investment markets is:*
   1. They will always be too risky.
   2. If I'm careful, there will be opportunity.
   3. There is always lots of upside potential if you know what you're doing and aren't afraid to act.

M. If the value of your mutual fund went down by 10% this year even as other funds were going up, would you:
1. Continue to hold it?
2. Monitor it closely over the next year and sell if it continued to lose value?
3. Sell it and find one with better returns?

N. How many months of current expenses could you cover without dipping into your investable assets?
1. Six months to a year.
2. Less than six months.
3. One month or less.

Scoring:

Add the numbers circled and compare to the guide below.

You scored 14–20 . . . You're an ultra-conservative investor who rarely takes chances with money. Unless you have a very long time horizon or already control substantial wealth, you may want to try to nudge yourself to be less risk-averse to meet your retirement needs. Fear of short-term loss could lead you to forfeit a good deal of return needlessly.

You scored 21–30 . . . You're a middle-of-the-road investor who appreciates the need to take calculated risks. This is a good mind-set to have when investing for retirement.

You scored 31–42 . . . You're an aggressive investor who may get an emotional charge out of taking a risk.

You need to make sure that your inclination to do *something* in times of stress doesn't lead you to make unwise choices.

So what kind of investor are you? Nervous? High-Rolling? Or something in between? Whatever your instincts, you can achieve both comfort and safety with the right investment strategy.

I think *Buckets of Money*® is just such a strategy. Invest your money in short-term, mid-term, and long-term "buckets" and you'll likely:

- get the safe, reliable income you want from the very first year—and continuing for many years to come, perhaps as long as you live.
- increase your income periodically to keep pace with inflation; and
- produce a substantial portfolio that you can continue to live on, or that you pass onto your heirs.

And Buckets is flexible. If your tolerance for risk is higher or lower than usual, if your need for an income stream is more or less than somebody else's, if you want to get by on less in the short term in order to reap more down the road, or vice versa, the *Buckets of Money*® system can be tweaked to match your preferences.

I'll give you plenty of examples of how Buckets works. But they will only be that—*examples*. At the end of the next chapter, there will be a worksheet where you can plug in your own numbers.

Whatever numbers you chose, I think you'll see the simple logic of this strategy. While no one can guarantee results, the *Buckets of Money*® plan provides the best chance of any strategy I've seen to give you both comfort and safety.

Short Term - bucket
Income bucket

Chapter 4

BUCKETS:
THE SIMPLE, YET PROVEN, SYSTEM

Here's a safe gamble: I'm willing to bet that you, unlike the Nervous Nelsons or the High-Rolling Hendersons, don't want to go broke slowly *or* quickly. Am I right? *See!* What a guy!

You want to invest soundly, conservatively. You don't want to bet the farm on the short-term gyrations of an erratic stock market. But neither do you wish to invest so timidly that inflation erodes your nest egg. So how can you do both: receive income *and* get the growth that stocks and other long-term investments can bring?

That's where the Buckets come into play. Think of them as the short-term bucket (No. 1, the "Income" bucket), mid-term (No. 2, the "Safety" bucket), and long-term buckets (No. 3, the "Growth" bucket). You'll want to split your money, putting some into each bucket. The worksheet calculator at the end of this chapter will guide you through the fairly simple calculations.

How you divide the money will depend on (a) how much you have to invest, (b) how much income you will need to live on and when you need it, (c) how many years you need that income for, and (d) what rate of return and rate of inflation you predict.

But for purposes of our example, let's say you, like the Nelsons and the Hendersons, have $300,000 to invest and need income of $18,000 a year. This is also the example used on the worksheet calculator, so you can follow along there if you wish.

In the short-term Bucket No. 1, you would need to put about $104,000 and invest that in something very safe that will produce $18,000 annually for seven years. (For our example, we assume a 5% return for Bucket No. 1.) This can be done by investing in short-term instruments like CDs, or Treasury bills or Treasury notes with laddered maturities. Investing in an immediate annuity also will provide you with guaranteed, tax-favored income for a specific period. (In Chapters 5–7, we will go into much more detail about the kinds of investments that will be best for each bucket.)

A key point

A key here is that—probably contrary to what you've heard or read—you will draw down not only the interest on this Bucket No. 1 money, *but the principal, too.* (Some people have a problem with that; they've always been told that's a no-no. But, trust me, in this case, it's O.K., and in fact, it's necessary to make the Buckets plan work.) However, you will not touch the other buckets until Bucket No. 1 is dry.

In the second, or "Safety" bucket, you would put $85,000, and let it grow for the seven years while Bucket No. 1 is churning out income. The Bucket No. 2 money is also invested for safety, but can handle slightly more risk and provide more hope of reward than the money in the first bucket. In our example, we use a conservative 6% figure for the return from funds in the second bucket. So at that rate, the $85,000 will grow to more than $128,000 by the time Bucket No. 1 has run dry, seven years from now. (You don't *really* let it run dry . . . but I'll get into that later.)

Then what?

At the end of the seven years, you pour the $128,000 into the empty Bucket No. 1. Bucket No. 2 is empty and stays empty until it's eventually re-filled by Bucket No. 3. Meanwhile, Bucket No. 1 begins pouring out money for the next seven-year cycle.

But, remember, a major goal of the Buckets strategy is to keep pace with inflation. So in this next seven-year period (years 8 through 14), you will need more income to buy the same amount of goods and services. Thus, you draw $22,000 a year (instead of $18,000) for the second seven years.

So far, then, you've gotten 14 years of safe income, adjusted for inflation. But what's happening to the yet-untouched Bucket No. 3?

The growth bucket

Because you put $104,000 of your $300,000 in Bucket No. 1 and $85,000 in Bucket No. 2, that leaves almost $111,000 for the third bucket. You're not counting on this bucket for income to live on. And you can wait a long time (up to 14 years in this example) before needing to draw on Bucket No. 3. So you can take some risk by putting that money in the stock market and other more high-risk, high-return investments.

You'll recall from Chapter 2 that I explained how stock-market risk lessens greatly with time. So putting some dough in the stock market, then ignoring it is a very sound strategy. Or, as I like to say . . .

Lucia's Law   **17**

Ignoring the market's ups and downs can, over time, make you a pile of money.

Fourteen years should be enough time for some of the market's fluctuations to balance out. With any kind of luck, that should be long enough for you to get pretty decent returns.

The Standard & Poors 500, the most closely-followed general market index, tells us that stocks have generated better than a 10% rate of return over the last 70 years or so. Understand, this is *not* guaranteed. But if the stock market is as investor-friendly in the future as it has been in the past and generates about 10%, the nearly $111,000 in Bucket No. 3 will have grown to more than $420,000 after 14 years.

Managing your Bucket relationships

I simplified the above scenario to show how the three buckets differ in their goals and how they're invested. In real life, though, the buckets are not independent of one another. You don't treat them as self-contained entities to be emptied one after another.

Instead, the Buckets must work in tandem: income-safety-growth. For example, let's say your Bucket No. 3 investments were growing at 10%, higher than the 8% you had projected. You could take the excess and add it to your Bucket No. 2. That would be taking money from growth (Bucket No. 3) to ensure that there's always safe money (Bucket No. 2) available for income (Bucket No. 1).

Conversely, if a bear market caused Bucket No. 3's growth to slow, a sophisticated investor might even want to take money from Bucket No. 2 to replenish the growth bucket.

But here's the rule: You don't ever want an *empty* Bucket No. 2. You never want to go directly from growth (Bucket No. 3) to income (Bucket No. 1) because no one knows when the next bear market will occur. One of the worse things any investor can do is run out of safe money and be forced to liquidate stocks for income in a down market. After all, that's what got the High-Rolling Hendersons into trouble.

Regularly, probably on an annual basis, you ought to take a look at how each bucket is doing and reallocate among the three. Any excess from Bucket No. 3 should end up in Bucket No. 2. And any extra Bucket No. 2 money can be "banked" where it is or could flow into Bucket No. 1 to extend its life. You should *always* have, say, at least a couple years' income in Bucket No. 2

Making sure you have sufficient money in Bucket Nos. 1 and 2 is a way of buying time. And, of course, buying time is at the heart of the whole *Buckets of Money*® strategy: The longer you can leave your money in stocks and real estate, the better your chance of earning a healthy return. And making sure you have enough income and safe money is the way you allow Bucket No. 3 to grow.

A review

Let's go back and summarize what the *Buckets of Money*® can do for your retirement. First, regardless of the amount of money you have to invest, a Buckets plan can—if current assumptions hold true—provide you with a steady, reliable income. What's more, this income (as you empty Bucket No. 2 into Bucket No 1) can be adjusted to keep pace with inflation. That's what I call "comfort," and it's what the Nervous Nelsons failed to achieve.

Second, Buckets will allow you to draw your income confidently, knowing that the amounts you need to live on are coming from diversified investments, which, as you'll remember from Chapter 2, is better than just relying on one investment source. That's what I call "safety," and that's what the High-Rolling Hendersons failed so miserably at.

Third, at the end of 14 years (in our example), the strategy produces a portfolio of stocks and other long-term investments that potentially could be worth much more than your entire original nest egg ($300,000 becoming $420,000 in our example.)

What if?

What if you have more than $300,000 to invest? You can divvy it up in ways to give you more income (putting more into Buckets Nos. 1 and 2) and/or more growth (putting more into Bucket No. 3).

Or if you can wait more than 14 years, you can let your third bucket continue to grow. Or if you get lucky and there's a higher rate of return or lower rate of inflation, that, too, would affect the amounts you'll have to work with. The worksheet calculator allows you to fiddle with various scenarios.

I personally like retirees to attempt to live on 4% to 5% of their assets rather than 6%–8%. Although the higher numbers are do-able, the chance for success dramatically increases as you lower your requirement for income or lower the inflation rate.

Then what?

What do you do at the end of the 14 years? Well, your first two buckets are probably running lean, although you should always have at least some safe money—perhaps a couple years' worth on hand.

But the bulk of your money, by far, is in Bucket No. 3. So you can take your stock portfolio and use this sum to . . .

- start filling the buckets all over again, generating an even higher, inflation-adjusted income.
- care for yourself in your last years.
- cover the costs of emergencies or large expenses.
- give to your favorite charities.
- make gifts to your children or grandchildren.
- pass on a substantial sum to your heirs after you're gone.

Or, for that matter, for *any* purpose you choose. The important thing is that as you grow older, while others may have to make do with less and less, you, having mastered the *Buckets of Money*® strategy, will be growing *stronger* and *more secure*.

But what about a parachute?

You're probably thinking: "So far, so good. Sounds reasonable in theory. But what if I break an ankle and can't work for a couple months? Or a tornado takes the roof off the house and the insurance company drags its feet? Or my daughter suddenly decides to get married and wants a big wedding? Or my car goes totally kaput? I'll need money—and *quick*—but it'll all be tied up in those danged buckets."

Well, no, it won't. Those kinds of unplanned expenses *do* happen. And sometimes it isn't even a small disaster but a chance to do something enjoyable—take a brief, spur-of-the-moment vacation, say, or replace that faded carpeting before the holidays—that requires a short-term cash infusion. What you're going to need is a parachute, if you will, in case your financial plane runs into such turbulence.

This sum will be a lot smaller than a bucket—so let's call it a "cup." Everybody needs a cup of money stashed away. (Maybe you already have set some aside in a "rainy day" fund.) How big a cup? That will depend on the level and stability of your other income. If you're in a business where layoffs are common, for instance, you'll want to put more away than the guy who teaches school. If you've got money coming in from, say, a pension, Social Security, or real estate, you might not need as much as somebody else whose salary is his sole income. Your tolerance for risk also will dictate how big your cup of money needs to be.

Usually, an emergency cup of three to four months of your normal spending needs is sufficient. This cash must be instantly accessible—not in a retirement account where you might face big taxes or a withdrawal penalty. And you don't want to have to drain money out of your three investment buckets.

Often this money resides in a money-market or other safe account, such as a CD or even a bond fund. But the point is, when implementing the *Buckets of Money*® strategy, it's just as important to select the proper vehicle for these emergency funds as it is for the sums being invested in the buckets.

Most people keep their emergency fund for the rest of their life because though they may have an occasional unplanned, big expense, they don't have so many of them that this fund is depleted. If they don't have any really serious setbacks, this fund may ultimately pass onto their heirs. Thus, this money is often also referred to as the Legacy Asset. Ironically, the most common use of the emergency-fund money is paying for long-term convalescent care.

We'll talk in the next chapter about what kinds of assets are best for your cup. But, for now, just understand that there's nothing about the Buckets plan that will prevent you from being able to deal with short-term emergencies. *There,* feel better?

What's your plan?

Now it's your turn to figure out how to best divide your investable assets. I've used our $300,000/14-year scenario as an example on the following worksheet calculator. The tables that accompany the calculator assume you're going to retire in one year. (If you're retiring earlier than that, a slightly different set of tables would apply. But because I'm trying to give you a general idea here—not teach a math class—these tables will probably be close enough for your purposes and mine.)

Remember that the goal was to provide a seven-year income stream of $18,000 annually from Bucket No.1, then in the eighth year, increase the income to cover inflation. Keep in mind that the reason I used a seven-year period for both Bucket No. 1 and another seven-year time period for Bucket No. 2 was to illustrate a very conservative approach, one that should work over just about any 14-year period. A look back at the history suggests it would take the mother of all bear markets to seriously unsettle a stock portfolio after 14 years of owning good companies and reinvesting dividends.

More aggressive investors may want to use a five- or six-year time frame for each bucket. In that case, you can easily modify the numbers by funding fewer dollars in Buckets Nos.1 and 2 and more into growth in Bucket No. 3. If the equity markets perform at historical norms, you might end up with a significantly better rate of return and a much bigger Bucket No. 3 after the first two buckets are emptied.

But for your sake, I prefer to err on the conservative side. So let's stick with seven-year buckets for the purposes of this example. Also, it should be noted that in some instances Bucket No. 1 will need to be stair-stepped to account for other income available at a later date. For example, an individual age 60 and two years away from receiving Social Security, may want to bolster Bucket No. 1

to support a higher income needed for the next two years. It is simple math, thus any variations should be quick and easy to calculate.

We'll go into this in more detail in subsequent chapters, but understand that certain investments or investment strategies are clearly more appropriate for some buckets than for others. For example, you wouldn't want to place any stocks or equity mutual funds in Bucket No. 1. It would be far too risky to draw out principal and interest from a stock portfolio that could suffer a substantial market correction without warning. Also, you would certainly not want cash investments—like CDs or money-market funds—in Bucket No. 3 because they have so little long-term growth potential.

It's your turn

Assume you're one year away from retirement, then plug in your projections. You'll probably want to experiment with different amounts, time periods, and rates of return and inflation. *Good luck!*

After you've entered your specific goals and projections, you'll have a general idea of what you can realistically expect from your portfolio at retirement. Once that's done, the easy stuff is out of the way. Tackling the numerous investment options, analyzing the impact of taxes and determining which buckets are most appropriate for the various investment strategies takes a bit more work. That's next.

PLAN YOUR OWN FUTURE WITH BUCKETS OF MONEY®

		Example	**You**
Starting point: Your total investable assets today	**(1)**	$300,000.00	_____

STEP 1: How much do you put into Bucket #1?

Multiply desired monthly income. *Example:* $1,500 [your choice: $_____] × *12* = annual income

	(2)	18,000.00	_____

Go to **Table A** at the end of this worksheet. Along the left margin are Number of Years. Along the top are Rates. Select the Number of Years you want to get Income from Bucket #1. *Example:* 7 years [your choice: ____ years] and the rate of return you expect to earn from risk-fee investments such as CDs, immediate annuities, Treasury bills or money-market funds. *Example:* 5% [your choice: ____%]

71

With your finger, follow the
line of numbers from the year
you've chosen until you're
under the rate you want.
Enter on Line 3 the number
you find there   **(3)**   × 5.7864   _____

Multiply the number on
Line 3 times your desired
annual income (Line 2). This
is the amount you need to
put into Bucket #1 today.
Write it on Line 4   **(4)** $104,155.20   _____

STEP 2: How much do you put into Bucket #2?

First calculate how inflation will affect your income needs.

Enter your annual income
from Bucket #1 (Line 2)   **(5)**   18,000.00   _____

What do you think the average rate of inflation will be
during the period you selected in Step 1? *Example:* 3% [your
choice: ____%]

Now go to **Table B.** Find the
Number of Years you selected
in Step 1 and follow that line
across to the rate of inflation
you just chose. Write the

number you find there on
Line 6   **(6)**   1.2299   _____

Now multiply it by Line 5.The
result is the annual income
you'll need after Bucket #1 is
empty   **(7)**   22,138.20   _____

Now multiply this by the num-
ber you used in Line 3   **(8)**   × 5.7864   _____

The result is the amount of
money Bucket #2 must con-
tain by the time Bucket #1
is empty   **(9)** $128,100.48   _____

To calculate how much you need to put into Bucket #2
today, answer this: What rate of return can you expect
from conservative investments during the period you chose
in Step 1? *Example:* 6% [your choice: ____%]

Go back to Table B, select the
Bucket #1 time period, follow
that line across to the rate you
just entered. Write the number
you find there on Line 10 **(10)**   ÷ 1.5036   _____

Divide the number on Line 10
into the amount on Line 9.
This is how much you need
to put into Bucket #2 today.
Write it on Line 11   **(11)** $85,195.85   _____

STEP 3: How much is left for Bucket #3?

Enter total investable assets
from Line 1   **(12)** $300,000.00   _____

SUBTRACT the amount you're
putting into Bucket #1 today
(Line 4)   **(13)**   −104,155.20   _____

ALSO SUBTRACT the amount
you're putting into Bucket #2
today (Line 11)   **(14)**   − 85,195.85   _____

The result is the amount you
have left over to put into
Bucket #3 today. Write it on
Line 15   **(15)** $110,648.95   _____

To calculate how much you can expect this figure to grow, ask yourself what rate of return you can expect from a diversified stock portfolio during the two periods you'll be getting income from Buckets #1 and #2. *Example:* 10% [your choice: ____%]

Go back to Table B, select the total time in the two periods you're taking from Buckets #1 and #2 and follow that line across to the rate you just entered.

Write the number you find
there on Line 16   **(16)**   3.7975   _____

Now multiply that number by
Line 15 and write the answer
on Line 17   **(17)** $420,189.38   _____

If your assumptions hold true, this is the amount you can
expect will be in Bucket #3 when you're ready to start drawing from it.

***RESULT: Using our conservative assumptions, and start-
ing with $300,000, you would have a safe, inflation-
adjusted income for 14 years and an ending value of
more than $420,000 with which to start the Buckets of
Money® strategy all over again.***

TABLE A

Years	4%	5%	6%	7%	8%	9%	10%
5	4.4518	4.3295	4.2124	4.1002	3.9927	3.8897	3.7908
6	5.2421	5.0757	4.9173	4.7665	4.6229	4.4859	4.3553
7	6.0021	5.7864	5.5824	5.3893	5.2064	5.0330	4.8684
8	6.7327	6.4623	6.2098	5.9713	5.7466	5.5348	5.3349
9	7.4353	7.1078	6.8017	6.5152	6.2469	5.9952	5.7590
10	8.1109	7.7217	7.3601	7.0236	6.7101	6.4177	6.1446

TABLE B

Years	3%	4%	5%	6%	7%	8%	9%	10%	12%
6	1.1941	1.2653	1.3401	1.4185	1.5007	1.5869	1.6771	1.7716	1.9738
7	1.2299	1.3159	1.4071	1.5036	1.6058	1.7138	1.8280	1.9487	2.2107
8	1.2668	1.3686	1.4775	1.5938	1.7182	1.8509	1.9926	2.1436	2.4760
9	1.3048	1.4233	1.5513	1.6895	1.8385	1.9990	2.1719	2.3579	2.7731
10	1.3439	1.4802	1.6289	1.7980	1.9672	2.1589	2.3674	2.5937	3.1058
11	1.3842	1.5395	1.7103	1.8983	2.1049	2.3316	2.5804	2.8531	3.4785
12	1.4258	1.6010	1.7959	2.0122	2.2522	2.5182	2.8127	3.1384	3.8960
13	1.4685	1.6651	1.8856	2.1329	2.4098	2.7196	3.0658	3.4523	4.3635
14	1.5126	1.7317	1.9799	2.2609	2.5785	2.9372	3.3417	3.7975	4.8871
15	1.5580	1.8009	2.0789	2.3966	2.7590	3.1722	3.6425	4.1722	5.4736
16	1.6047	1.8730	2.1829	2.5404	2.9522	3.4259	3.9703	4.5950	6.1304
17	1.6528	1.9479	2.2920	2.6928	3.1588	3.7000	4.3276	5.0545	6.8660
18	1.7024	2.0258	2.4066	2.8543	3.3799	3.9960	4.7171	5.5599	7.6900
19	1.7535	2.1068	2.5270	3.0256	3.6165	4.3157	5.1417	6.1159	8.6128
20	1.8061	2.1911	2.6533	3.2071	3.8697	4.6610	5.6044	6.7275	9.6463

Chapter 5

THE FIRST BUCKET: CONSISTENT, GUARANTEED, TAX-FAVORED INCOME

How much risk do you want to take with your Bucket No. 1, the short-term bucket that's going to sustain you while the other two grow?

Try *zero.*

Here you want to take a page from the Nervous Nelsons' book and think *safety.* (Unlike the Nelsons, though, you're only putting *a part* of your nest-egg into ultra-conservative investments, not the whole thing.)

You don't want to worry about your monthly retirement check. Thus, you probably want to limit choices in Bucket No. 1 to only very safe investments. That means: little, if any, price fluctuation and virtually no chance of losing any principal.

As we learned in Chapter 3, risk tolerance varies from investor to investor. Each person/couple will have to make his/their own decisions about how much risk they are willing to accept in Bucket No. 1. But the most prudent choice—and what I recommend—is that you take zero risk.

In this chapter, we're going to survey the kinds of investments that would work for Bucket No. 1 and spell out their pros and cons.

Vary from time to time

Understand that those pros and cons change with the times. The attractiveness of many investments wax and wane depending on what's happening with interest rates and how aggressive lending institutions and insurance companies are acting at the moment. Some times, for example, bonds are the best choice. Other times CDs and fixed annuities may lead the pack.

So what's best this year may not be best next year. This is where your financial advisor can help you make the correct bucket choices. (See Chapter 10 for ideas on how to find the right financial planner for you.)

Bucket No. 1 Possibilities

❑ **Immediate annuity.** What you want from your Bucket No. 1 is convenient and hassle-free retirement income. An Immediate Annuity Contract (IAC) is just that: It delivers a check to your door each month or automatically deposits it to your checking account on the same date, month in and month out.

An IAC is a great way to go if you don't want to deal with reinvesting interest every six months from a bond portfolio, or shopping among banks for the best interest rates when your CDs mature, or dealing with brokers, or, worse yet, dealing with the government. In short, IACs amount to a "no brainer"—a very safe and dependable source of retirement income.

What exactly is it?

An immediate annuity is a contract issued by an insurance company guaranteeing payments of a specific sum to a retiree each month on a specific date. This can last for either a fixed number of months, or for the rest of the annuitant's life or the life of the joint annuitants. For *Buckets* planning, of course, it only makes sense to use an annuity that pays out principal and interest over a fixed number of months.

For instance, if you want $1,500 deposited into your checking account on the 15th of each month for the next seven years (the projected term of our Bucket No. 1), an insurance company will ask you to pay a lump sum equal to the discounted present value of that benefit amount based on the current interest rates they are crediting. If the insurer is currently crediting 4% net after expenses, a $1,500 monthly payment for 84 months would call for a single, up-front premium of $109,739.

In other words, your $109,739 buys you $1,500 per month for seven years, or 84 months, *guaranteed!* This includes *both* the principal and the interest. At the end of 84 months, all the money in the IAC will have been used up.

But suppose interest rates are higher, meaning the insurance company can get a better return on the lump sum you hand over. If the insurer credits a net 6%, then the amount required from you to fund the $1,500 payment for 84 months declines to $102,680, or about $7,000 less.

So, obviously, an IAC is more attractive at some times than others. Further, some states require insurance companies to pay a state premium tax on immediate annuities. This can cause the actual return on your investment to be a bit lower than other suitable Bucket No. 1 investment possibilities. That's a downside.

But the big advantages of IACs include their imposed discipline as well as convenience. In my view, those two plusses are unmatched and may be worth a slightly lower rate of return. For ease of budgeting, IACs are hard to beat. You usually can choose the day of the month to receive your annuity payment. Thus, you can coordinate that check with your Social Security check and/or your pension checks and have all of them deposited in your bank account each month on or about the same day.

Some contend that a fixed, immediate annuity is somewhat restrictive because it requires the retiree to live on a budget. That's true.

But I would argue such a limitation can be good. If Bucket No. 1 funds were readily available, you might be tempted to spend more than you should. Then you'd be forced to dip into your other buckets, and this could upset your long-term financial security. (Also, remember, our emergency "cup"—that exists for special needs.)

Here's another advantage of IACs: You can claim your hands are tied when friends or relatives hit you up for cash. While it is indeed a noble gesture to help your "neighbor," you should keep in mind . . .

Lucia's Law — **18**

Toss your cash into a tornado . . . and the chances of seeing it again are about the same as that of recovering loans to family or friends.

Sad to say, I've learned this from personal experience. (Again, remember you've got the emergency cup. It's there to lend a helping hand if you must.) But an immediate annuity can help you—with sincerity and conviction—to "Just Say 'No.'"

In truth, some immediate annuity contracts are liquid. But you don't have to advertise that fact. It's easier just to say your money is tied up in a "retirement plan" and unavailable. Over the years, I have saved many clients from bad investments in family restaurants, jojoba ranches, ostrich farms, and other ventures of dubious merit because their retirement money was "tied up" in something perceived and accepted (perhaps with disappointment) by friends and relatives as illiquid.

Another benefit

Another major benefit of an immediate annuity in an after-tax personal account (not traditional IRAs, pensions, etc.) is something called the exclusion ratio. If you invest in CDs or government bonds, you are taxed on the full amount of the interest earned each year on the entire sum invested.

Because an immediate annuity pays out *both* principal and interest on a fully amortized basis, this dramatically reduces your current income-tax liability. With an immediate annuity you only pay tax on the pro-rata amount of interest you receive in the year you receive it. The rest of the interest is deferred until it is withdrawn in subsequent years.

Here's an example: If you deposit $109,739 with an insurance company and receive $1,500 in monthly income payments over 84 months, you actually receive a total of $126,000 over the seven-year period, $16,261 of which is interest. If you divide the $16,261 interest by seven years you get $2,323 per year. That is the amount of interest you need to report each year on your tax return. In the 28% tax bracket, the immediate annuity will only cost you about $650 in federal taxes per year on $18,000 of income ($2,323 $\times$ .28). In contrast, your first-year federal tax liability on $5,000 of interest income (from, say, CDs or Treasuries) would be about $1,800.

If you were to ignore the *Buckets of Money*® concept, draw a $1,500 monthly income from just the interest from a bond fund or CD, you would need to deposit $300,000 (assuming you earned 6%). Further, all $18,000 earned per year would be taxable, leaving an individual in a 28% marginal tax bracket a spendable income of $12,960. This is significantly less than the $17,350 of spendable cash you would have generated from an immediate annuity. In fact, with the IAC you'd have 33% more money to initially spend at retirement.

Of course, with the annuity you are using principal and interest. But that's O.K. because Bucket No. 3 is left to grow and in most instances will more than make up for the principal exhausted in Bucket No. 1.

Annuities also help when it comes to figuring out how much of your Social Security benefits will be subject to tax. When a single individual's modified adjusted gross income (MAGI) reaches $32,000 and married couples MAGI exceeds $44,000, 85% of their Social Security benefits become taxable. If you are nearing those income levels, the immediate annuity can help you stay below the threshold and save even more tax.

So, let's summarize the pros and cons of IACs:

Pros
- Eases your budgeting. Safe and dependable, IACs deliver predictable income on predictable dates.

- Requires you to live within your means. By not having immediate access to your money you might think twice about those expenditures that exceed your regular budget.
- Gives you tax advantages. You only pay tax on the pro-rata amount of interest you receive in the year you receive it; the rest is deferred until it is withdrawn in subsequent years.
- May help avoid taxation of your Social Security benefits.
- Provides a ready excuse when friends or relatives come calling with their hands out.
- Is handled outside of probate at your death.

Cons
- Forces you to live on a "budget."
- May reduce your return because of taxes the insurer must pay on your premium in some states.

Clearly, there are a lot of advantages to IACs. But while they are excellent investments for safety, income and convenience, they are clearly not the only choice for a Bucket No.1. So let's move on!

❑ **Laddered-maturity Treasuries or laddered CDs.** One of the most popular ways to structure a Bucket No.1 guaranteed-income portfolio is to ladder investments, so a specified sum matures on the date you need it each year.

If, for example, you want $18,000 annually ($1,500 per month), the first step is to set up a check-writing money-market mutual fund. Once that's established, you then deposit the first year's income needs (approximately

$18,000) into the fund and each month write yourself a check for $1,500. At the end of the year, when your money fund has dried up, your first CD or Treasury instrument kicks in.

In a seven-year *Buckets* strategy the idea is to ladder six fixed investments, each maturing one year apart, starting at the beginning of year two and ending at the beginning of year seven. After that, it's time to empty Bucket No. 2.

Certificates of Deposit at your local bank are probably the easiest investments to ladder. However U.S. Treasury securities with comparable interest rates and maturities have a slight advantage if you live in an area with a state income tax. That's because government securities (held by you personally, not in traditional IRA or pension accounts) are exempt from state income tax, but CDs are not.

Thus, your net after-tax return could be slightly higher with Treasuries. But it may not be worth the extra effort. That's because you either have to deal with a broker, who will most likely charge you a fee to arrange the purchase, or you deal directly with a Federal Reserve Bank online or through the mail. Either way, the amount of additional interest you would earn is marginal. So opting for convenience may make the most sense.

Another excellent place to shop for fixed-interest laddered maturity investments is a credit union. Sometimes credit unions will offer members interest rates slightly above that of bank CDs and short-term Treasury securities. So credit unions are definitely worth checking out.

But whether you use banks, money market mutual funds, short-term Treasuries, credit unions or immediate annuities, the yields should be comparable and your principal should be very safe.

Again, let's look at the pros and cons of laddering:

Pros:
- Safe and dependable.
- Flexible. You set up the schedule, and you're not forced to live on a "budget."
- Tax advantages. If you chose Treasury securities, you may save on state income tax.
- Credit unions may have special rates for members.

Cons
- Some fees and/or paperwork required if you chose Treasury securities.
- Interest on CDs not tax exempt.

❏ **Short-term bond mutual funds.** Another low-risk investment for Bucket No. 1—and perhaps the simplest to fund—is a short-term-bond mutual fund. These funds invest primarily in short-term government securities that mature in one to five years. The reason they are so simple is the mutual fund company makes all the investment decisions for you.

Instead of you having to shop for CDs and Treasuries or pick the right bond investments at the right time, a portfolio manager does it for you (for a nominal fee.) You simply ask the bond fund company to send you a monthly income check from the account.

Here's the way it works: The fund company withdraws the interest from your account first, and then it sells shares of the mutual fund in your account to meet your target income. Yields on short-term bond funds will be similar to CDs or Treasuries, perhaps even marginally higher depending on how seasoned the underlying bonds are in the portfolio and what happens to interest rates. If there are bonds in the mutual fund portfolio with higher-than-market yields and interest rates are inching lower, then you may even pick up an extra return by using a short-term bond fund over other, less risky portfolio alternatives. (Not that short-term bond funds are that risky, it's just that they're not guaranteed.) When interest rates are low, the yields on short-term bond mutual funds will also be lower, because as the higher interest rate bonds mature, newer, lower-yielding bonds are purchased, and the fund's yield declines.

While simple, easy, and potentially higher yielding, bond funds may not produce the best result for Bucket No.1. The prices of bonds and bond mutual funds fluctuate each day based on the daily direction of interest rates. The share price of short-term bonds and bond funds fluctuate less than longer-term bond mutual funds, but they *do* change.

In periods of rising interest rates, the share price can decline faster than the benefit derived by a little higher interest rate. If this happens and shares must be sold at a loss, the return on Bucket No.1 may become unacceptably low, and, shorten the length of Bucket No. 1's pay-out. At the end of the day a Bucketeer will have to choose between the absolute safety of potentially lower-yielding CDs, Treasuries, or immediate annuities and the potentially higher-yielding mutual fund whose value may decline enough to erase some of the benefit of higher initial returns.

Price fluctuation aside, there is a small chance of losing any principal in highly rated, short-term bonds or bond funds. It usually comes down to comparing the options at the time you are ready to invest and seeking the best yield at that time. Bonds may fit Bucket No. 1 best when interest rates are high and expected to remain reasonably stable throughout most of Bucket No. 1's payout period, rather than when rates are low with the possibility of higher rates ahead.

To recap short-term bond funds:

Pros:
- Very simple to administer. No shopping required.
- Low risk. Chances of losing principal are slight.
- Similar yields to CDs and Treasuries.

Cons:
- Some price fluctuation.
- Not as attractive when interest rates are low and headed upward.

Those three investments—immediate annuities, laddered CDs or Treasuries, and short-term bond funds—are what I see as best for Bucket No. 1. Though there are differences among them, they all offer safe, consistent income. Further, that income stream requires relatively little effort by you to keep it flowing. So, they offer safety and security. And, after all, that's what you're seeking in Bucket No. 1.

A couple less attractive possibilities

Two other possibilities are worth discussing, though for reasons you'll soon see, they're not in the same league with our Big Three.

❑ **Mid- and long-term-bonds or bond funds.** Brokers wanting to enhance their client's return may be tempted to opt for higher-yielding mid-term or longer-term bonds, or long-term bond mutual funds. Unlike shorter-maturity bonds, these can and often do lose principal value if interest rates rise.

Thus, I feel longer-term bonds are usually *not* appropriate as a Bucket No. 1 investment. Rising interest rates can cause your principal in a bond or bond fund to decline substantially. That's not good in any situation, but it's doubly bad when (as with Bucket No. 1) you're systematically withdrawing funds to live on. Taking money out of a declining asset base can be frightening, especially if the declining asset represents your entire nest egg.

For instance, in 1994, interest rates increased 2%. Most bonds and bond funds suffered a significant principal loss for the year. While the loss was recovered in subsequent years as interest rates plummeted, retirees who were withdrawing cash from their long-term bond fund lost money on that portion of their portfolio forever. Once again in 1999, long-term-bond investors lost 12% of their principal as interest rates rose. Remember, there's no assurance that interest rates will decline so investors can recover that loss in short order.

If the economy experiences an inflationary spiral like it did in the late 1970s and early 1980s when interest rates rose consistently throughout the decade, substantial principal could be lost in bonds and bond mutual funds. Such losses hardly make retirees comfortable, especially when they see their principal disappear before their very eyes in an investment that is supposed to be safe.

What's more, remember, the *Buckets of Money*® concept requires a total depletion of a conservative Bucket No. 1. That buys you time to invest for additional safety and moderate growth in Buckets No. 2 and No. 3. The only way to buy that needed time is to deplete some of your principal using Bucket No. 1 assets and reinvest Bucket No. 2 assets based on your tolerance for risk.

But if you extract an income stream consisting of principal and interest from an investment that is losing value, you accelerate the loss. Or, as I have been known to say . . .

Lucia's Law | 19

Drawing down an already-failing asset is like throwing water on a sinking ship—it just goes to the bottom that much faster.

The withdrawals mean the principal produces less interest, and as you continue to withdraw, the whole investment spirals downward. As a result, Bucket No. 1 won't last as long as you planned, and that's going to throw off your whole *Buckets* plan.

So attempting to improve the interest return on Bucket No. 1 by extending the maturities on bonds or bond funds only to gain a .5 to 1% advantage can be foolish. (However, midterm and longer-term investments are just what you're looking for in Bucket No. 2, which we'll cover in the next chapter.)

The big picture on mid- and long-term bonds and bond funds looks like this:

Pros
- Slightly higher returns.

Cons
- Can lose principal if interest rates rise.
- Can subvert *Buckets of Money*® principle by forcing you to deplete Bucket No. 1 faster than intended.

❑ **A hybrid approach: money-market and bond funds.** Bucketeers sophisticated enough to handle their own investing—and willing to assume modest risk—may want to consider a hybrid approach to funding Bucket No. 1. It is not automatic like IAC payments or systematic redemptions from a short-term bond mutual fund, laddered Treasuries, or CDs. But a hybrid approach will produce a higher-rate return *most*—but not all—of the time with a measured increase in the amount of risk.

This "hybrid" requires some work on your part. The idea is to pair a liquid, check-writing money market mutual fund with a higher-yielding, higher-risk bond fund, REIT, or a combination of the two. The strategy is to deplete one account *or* the other, depending on what happens with interest rates.

For example: If Bucket No. 1 requires $120,000, consider placing $60,000 in a money market account and $60,000 into higher-yielding securities. The money-market rates at this writing yield about 3% (with virtually no principal risk). A strategic-income fund, high-yield bond fund, or Ginny Mae (mutual) fund, or REIT yields 6% to 8% (with some potential for loss). Thus, the blended yield is over 6%, which is significantly higher than other typical Bucket No. 1 assets.

If interest rates are stable or moving lower, the Bucketeer would withdraw the principal and interest needed for the monthly budget from the higher-yielding securities by taking the interest first, then liquidating enough shares to cover the balance needed. Because income-oriented securities tend to rise in value as interest rates decline, you would actually be selling off some profits. In other words, you would be selling high—when your investments have performed well.

If interest rates rise, these same securities usually will decline in value. If this happens, the investor would cease withdrawals from the declining assets and begin to take withdrawals from the safe money-market account, where there is no price fluctuation. This allows the interest from the securities account to be reinvested, thus buying more shares at lower prices and potentially enhancing your return.

Inflation and the accompanying higher interest rates are often corrected within two to three years. In this example, there is ample money in the money-market account to buy two to three years' worth of time before you have to tap into the higher-yield funds.

The hybrid strategy, it's hoped, would allow for a recovery as interest rates eventually float back to the start point. So by the time you begin to deplete the higher-risk fund, most or all of your principal is recovered. If interest rates don't come down within a reasonable period of time, you have the potential for some loss of principal. This hybrid approach might provide a return that can exceed the typical Bucket No. 1's short-term investment. In a *stable* interest rate environment, the hybrid should exceed typical Bucket No. 1 investment returns by 1% to 1.5% annually. Bucketeers will have to decide if the potential extra return warrants the extra risk and the extra work.

So, to sum up:

Pros:
- Higher returns most of the time.

Cons:
- Requires retiree to keep close tabs on interest rate, act accordingly.
- Some potential for loss of prinicpal.

The best strategy for you

As you can see, Bucket No.1 investing can be as simple as receiving a check each month from an insurance company or mutual fund, or it can be as complex as a hybrid strategy in which you nimbly decide which account to draw on, depending on what interest rates are doing. Your financial acumen and the time you are willing to commit to managing your investments will dictate the best strategy for you.

One of most difficult hurdles for Bucketeers is the concept of depleting the principal in Bucket No. 1. The old notion of never dipping into principal is logical for individuals attempting to protect their nest egg. But keep in mind that it has the opposite effect over time. Or as I like to say . . .

Lucia's Law | 20

Protect at all costs the principal in your income-producing account—and you'll end up with neither *principal nor income.*

As inflation erodes your purchasing power, your net spendable income actually decreases. Remember, $18,000 a couple decades from now will probably only buy half the amount of goods and services it does today. Thus, you need a growing asset base in order to provide an inflation-indexed income.

Your equity-based investments (what you will have in Bucket No. 3) grow, and your fixed investments (Bucket No. 1) don't. So you should deplete principal in Bucket No. 1 in order to allow ample time in Bucket No. 3 for equities to do what they do best. That leaves Bucket No 2 . . . and the next chapter.

The emergency "cup"

But what about that emergency fund we discussed in the last chapter? What are good investments for that sum? And how much of a sum do you need?

Well, the old law (made famous by a series of television ads a few years ago) is that you need six months' salary in an insured savings account. (Not surprisingly, it was banks and savings and loans that ran those ads.)

That's a bit extreme. That would mean putting many thousands of dollars there to be savaged by inflation and taxes . . . all the while awaiting emergencies that probably will never happen. Is that smart? N-o-o-o, I don't think so.

Three or four months is likely closer to the mark, and you will probably want to put it in a money-market and/or short-term bond fund. Those would give you more flexibility than a CD (because there are no penalties for early withdrawal) and will pay more interest than a savings account. Then if you have an actual emergency, you could write checks on the money-market account first because that wouldn't trigger a capital gain or loss, which, at the very least, will complicate your tax returns. (Using the bond fund will entail a capital gain or loss, but then the bond fund pays slightly better interest.)

Money is relatively easy to borrow now, especially in a margin account at a brokerage (with its relatively low interest rates) or through a home-equity loan (interest on which is tax-deductible). So, depending on your risk-comfort level, you could get by with even less than three months' worth of cash equivalents.

Most people keep their emergency fund for the rest of their life and hope it will outlast them and thus be passed onto their heirs. That's why I call this portion of retirement savings the "Legacy Asset." Only a very serious situation, such as the need to pay for long-term convalescent care, would cause you to draw down on the majority of this reserve. Aside from that or a similar event, it's likely that the Legacy Asset will sit untouched.

The insurance option

As financial planners, we sometimes recommend using a special type of insurance policy for the Legacy Asset. Such policies can provide a growing cash value *and* access to your money in case of an urgent need as well as tax-deferred and/or tax-free death benefits.

Convalescent care, home health care, and other potential needs may also be accommodated by this type of insurance that's available to certain qualified individuals. Careful consideration of the needs for both life-insurance and long-term health care is an important part of anyone's financial planning.

Another approach comes from *The Wall Street Journal* columnist Jonathan Clements, who says he keeps only a small amount of his emergency fund in cash, with the rest going into a stock mutual fund. "By putting my emergency money in stocks, I am not just preparing for the worst. I am also preparing for my retirement." Clements figures that because of the returns earned by stocks, his emergency reserve should grow to far more than six months' living expenses and eventually add to the comfort of his retirement.

That's not for everybody, and you need to do what's right for you. But as with the Buckets, the strategy with your cup should be to invest smartly, with an eye not only toward return but also toward achieving the comfort that you desire and deserve in your retirement.

Chapter 6

THE SECOND BUCKET:
MORE SAFE INCOME AND
AN INFLATION-HEDGE . . .
BUT A BETTER RETURN

If the buckets were like people, Bucket No. 1 would be Larry Lunchbox, the working stiff who scrapes and scrounges to keep the money coming in so there's food on the table and a roof over his family's head. He can't take any chances with his hard-won wages. So he focuses on the short-term and on just paying his bills. His time horizon: short.

Bucket No 2 is akin to Sammy Suburban, a Yuppie middle-manager. Though not rich, he's a little more comfortable and can kick back a bit. He still needs income, of course, but he can sock some money away and let it grow. So he can take on a bit more risk than Larry Lunchbox, and if a really red-hot investment opportunity presented itself, Sammy could decide to go for it. His time horizon: medium, or five to seven years in our example.

The third bucket is more like Tommy Trustfund, a rich layabout. He has all the time in the world—and all the fun! He doesn't have to worry about tomorrow or even the next five to seven years. He can buy whatever sound investment is likely to pay the best return . . . and then, freed of fretting about the market's ups and downs, he can watch in amazement as his wealth compounds. His time horizon: long, or about 14 years in our example.

In the last chapter we looked at what investments work best for Larry Lunchbox's first bucket. The best choices: immediate annuities, CDs, and short-term bond funds. But what's the best bet for our Sammy Suburban and Bucket No. 2? Mid-term and longer-term investments are inappropriate for a depletion account like Bucket No. 1. But they are *excellent* for Bucket No. 2 because they usually generate a higher return over time.

Again, you neither want nor need to take excessive risks with Bucket No. 2. You'll have plenty of risk and excitement when you invest your Bucket No. 3 money. So focusing on higher yielding *fixed*-income securities in Bucket No. 2 usually makes the most sense.

All investments are aimed at either producing income or growing in value, or both. Fixed-income securities— those designed to make regular payments to you—provide a reasonable degree of certainty that the money will be available when it is needed. They are safer than growth-oriented investments in the sense that these payments are more reliable than the hoped-for growth.

Furthermore, Bucket No. 2 can also be used to potentially enhance your overall rate of return by taking advantage of certain buying opportunities. For example, following almost every stock market correction in the last

50 years (with the exception of 1973–1974), there was a significant recovery over the ensuing six months to two years. Because we have bought ample time in Bucket No. 1, more aggressive investors may choose to divert some of their Bucket No. 2 money into Bucket No. 3 shortly after a steep stock-market decline. Thus, if the market rebounds, the return on that portion invested from Bucket No. 2 could dramatically outpace the fixed or semi-fixed return of Bucket No. 2. After the bounce back, one could pay back the money borrowed from Bucket No. 2 and leave the excess profits to grow in Bucket No. 3.

There are many income-producing options for Bucket No. 2. Let's look in detail at a few of the best ones.

Bucket No. 2 Possibilities

❑ **Tax-deferred fixed annuities.** I've spent many hours analyzing the best investments for Bucket No. 2, and I've concluded that, depending on the interest-rate environment and your tax bracket, Guaranteed Investment Contracts (GIC), or tax-deferred fixed annuities, often make an ideal Bucket No. 2 investment. But, naturally, it's a mixed bag.

First, some background. A fixed annuity is, in effect, a tax-deferred CD paying a fixed, usually high return that's typically adjusted annually or after a number of years. The annuity is sponsored by an insurance company instead of a bank *and* taxes are deferred each year on the profits you earn. Naturally, tax-deferred money grows more quickly than money that's taxed annually.

GICs and tax-deferred fixed annuity contracts offer an excellent blend of both safety and reasonably high yields when interest rates are low with the potential to move higher. Having an investment that performs well in a rising interest-rate environment is a great way to protect against interest-rate risk.

Conventional wisdom suggests if you want high yields and low volatility, bonds or bond funds make most sense. I respectfully dissent because that's often just not true.

Which reminds me of an old saying that I'll label . . .

Lucia's Law   **21**

*When interest rates rise, two things can happen . . .
and they're both* bad.

The two bad effects are: Stocks usually lose value and bond prices decline. Because stocks are reserved for long-term growth in Bucket No. 3 (more about that later), a conservative Bucketeer may feel most comfortable with assets that offer a yield competitive with intermediate bonds but without the price fluctuation. Unlike bonds, the yield on a GIC or tax-deferred fixed annuity usually gets better if interests rates rise. And, if interest rates decline, the GIC yields will also decline, but that's okay.

The reason that's O.K. is because as interest rates move lower, stock prices usually soar. Thus, Bucket No. 3 will more than make up for the lower yields on a GIC. GICs and fixed annuities also offer tax deferral. So in a personal (taxable) account, the taxes due on the interest is deferred until after Bucket No. 1 is depleted. At that time the annuity can be annuitized—that is, set up to provide a fixed sum at regular intervals. Thus, it'll produce an income to replace Bucket No. 1, and the taxes will be spread out over a period of years. If Bucket No. 2 is an IRA/pension/401(k), etc., the fund is already tax-deferred and will all be taken as ordinary income when paid out, regardless of whether you use a fixed annuity.

But even without the advantage of tax deferral, fixed annuities pay excellent interest rates and those rates respond quickly to changing economic conditions. Currently, longer-term and higher-risk bond funds yield between 5% and 7% with the downside potential to lose principal if interest rates rise.

In contrast, many insurance companies offer fixed annuities with annually renewable interest rates in that same 5%–7% range. Fixed annuities usually earn rates near that of 10-year Treasuries, or in some cases even above it. However, if interest rates inch upward, the credited rate on a fixed annuity contract would most likely renew at the higher market rate. And unlike 10-year Treasuries or other bonds, there is no downside principal risk. But there's no upside appreciation either if interest rates decline.

Thus, when interest rates are low, with the potential to move up, a fixed annuity is superior to a bond or a bond fund. When rates are high with the potential to move down (and if you can predict when interest rates will go up or down, let me—and the rest of the world—know), bonds may be a better choice.

Great complement to stocks

I like fixed annuities because they are a great comple-ment to a well-diversified stock portfolio, especially when interest rates are on the rise. However, many financial pundits and self-proclaimed money experts constantly beat down annuities as an investment. The reason: Most insurance company products are not understood.

Fixed annuities, unlike variable annuities, are no-frills investments. They usually do not have extra fees or charges (outside of a nominal contract charge) and no out-of-the-ordinary expenses. They do not provide any upside po-tential like variable annuities, no death benefits to speak of, and no potential to shift from safety to growth with one easy phone call. All the profit the insurance company makes on the sale of fixed annuities is priced into the in-terest rate they credit. If you don't like the rate, you don't buy the contract. Fixed annuities are like tax-deferred CDs paying a fixed, usually high-yielding interest rate. As long as investors understand they are buying a contract that shouldn't be touched for five to seven years due to a sur-render penalty and until after age 59½ due to federal and state penalty taxes, they usually can enjoy the higher re-turns and the comfort of having those returns pegged to market interest rates.

I tend to favor a GIC that locks in the rate for five to seven years instead of one in which the rates change annually. This way the insurance company can't entice you with a high rate in the first year, then once you're locked in, lower it to enhance the firm's profit.

A question commonly asked is how can insurance companies offer competitive, "bond-type" interest rates and little or no price volatility? The answer is insurance companies are in the business of assuming risk in return for guarantees. They take your investment dollars, guarantee a return consistent with the yield on most mid-term, fixed-income securities, and then they invest the money in higher-yielding, longer-term investments (assuming the interest-rate risk and the investment risk themselves.) Insurance companies have massive distribution forces, including agents, brokers, direct sales, and direct distributors. They are constantly bringing in new capital to be invested. Thus, going out longer on the yield curve to achieve a higher interest rate for their customers is not as risky for them as it is for you and me.

Insurance companies can, (with few historic exceptions, like Executive Life of California Insurance Company, First Capital, etc.) weather interest-rate cycles. If interest rates rise, they use new money to fund any current needs for capital and leave the older investors alone. (By the way, GICs are not a "Ponzi scheme," in which early investors are paid off with proceeds from the more recent ones. Instead, insurance companies use their entire portfolio to back their fixed annuities.) In addition, because of a draconian surrender penalty, insurance companies know they will keep your money for the length of the contract term and don't have to worry about liquidity for years. This enables them to make more money for themselves and in turn give you more.

Many insurance company's fixed annuities have constantly exceeded the rates of return credited on five-year CDs and 10-year Treasuries by .5% to 1%. These products have long-term track records to prove their competitiveness over the past 10, 15 and 20 years. This makes fixed annuities an excellent option for Bucket No. 2.

Why are they hated?

If fixed annuities and GICs pay interest rates competitive with high-rated bond funds and without the volatility, why do so many financial pundits despise them? For one thing, many critics confuse fixed annuities with variable annuities, which offer a family of tax-deferred separate accounts similar to mutual funds under the umbrella of an insurance contract.

Variable annuities are more complex investment vehicles that offer a number of benefits for a price. Many financial pundits do not understand the value you receive for the fees charged in a variable annuity. Later I'll discuss where variable annuities fit and where they don't.

Some individuals complain that annuities create a lot of ordinary income and no capital gain, which is taxed at lower rates. This is true. Both fixed and variable annuities defer the gain, which is taxed at ordinary-income rates when the money is withdrawn. However, fixed annuities are invested in Bucket No. 2 for safety, not necessarily for growth, and the earnings are meant to be spent within a few years, not accumulated over time. So the fact that there is an ordinary-income hit is less significant than the reason you buy them, which is to have a *safe,* high-yielding investment.

For reasons that elude me, some uninformed investors don't like to deal with insurance companies. Maybe that's because there are some products sold by unscrupulous insurance agents that are perceived to be inappropriate. But there are good and bad apples in every business, including the investment world.

But those bad apples should not brand fixed or variable annuities as bad. When interest rates are relatively low and the risk of owning longer-term bonds is high, then a fixed annuity might be a great solution. The only downsides of a fixed annuity are the surrender charge, the pre-age-59½ penalty, and the possibility that if the insurer went broke, your money could be lost.

The surrender charge is the way insurance companies recover their costs if you surrender the contract before it expires. Invest for five to seven years, and you earn a high return. But if you bail out early, you may have to pay a declining fee (*e.g.,* 6% after one year, 5% after two years, 4% after three years, etc.). Of course, if you bail out of a five-year CD, there's "a substantial penalty for early withdrawal." Where's the difference?

The pre-age-59½ penalty is irrelevant if you plan on spending your annuity money after you retire (post-59½). But what about the risk that the insurance company could go belly-up and take your dough with it? While that's very unlikely and has happened only a few times in history, it does mean you need to choose solid companies, as you would want to do with any investment.

Some also argue against GICs because a broker receives a commission if you buy a fixed annuity. But if you have enough income coming in from Bucket No. 1 and the interest rate being offered by the insurer on your fixed annuity in Bucket No. 2 is higher than other safe alternatives, why should you care? If a broker earns a commission for having sold you an excellent product, so what?

Commissions of equal or greater amounts are also paid on most bond funds. And unlike bond funds, GICs don't charge an ongoing management fee of ½% to 1% per year.

Be careful, though, because for the sake of a higher commission, some not-so-professional advisors representing marginal companies may attempt to bait you with high rates in the early years, locking you into lower rates in subsequent years. And you can't get out because of a long-term surrender penalty. This type of fixed annuity should be avoided at all cost.

However, well-chosen fixed annuities sold by honest financial advisors through excellent companies can be great, safe investments for Bucket No. 2, though not always and not for everyone. To summarize:

Pros:

- Usually higher yielding than CDs and Treasuries.
- Interest is tax-deferred.
- Principal is guaranteed.
- Interest payments usually increase if market interest rates rise.
- Complements well-diversified stock portfolio.

Cons:

- Interest payments usually decrease if market interest rates fall.
- Surrender charge levied if you cash in early as well as a tax-penalty if you cash in before age 59½.
- Could face loss of principal if company folds.

❑ **Bonds.** Bonds and bond funds really shine in some eras. For example, in the inflation-ridden 1970s and '80s when interest rates were high with the possibility of moving lower, bonds were an especially good choice.

And what is a bond? A bond is a loan. It can be a loan to the government, a loan to municipalities, a loan to high-rated corporations, or a loan to low-rated or un-rated companies or foreign entities. The yield, or rate of return, on all of these loans vary, depending on (1) the credit-worthiness of the borrower and (2) the time remaining until the loan is either called, or it matures and is paid off.

Among the options for Bucket No. 2 are corporate bonds, Series I bonds, junk bonds, preferred stocks, Ginny Maes, tax-free municipals, and even REITs. And some variable annuities also may qualify. Bonds pretty much pay a fixed return for a specific time and then upon maturity, your principal is returned.

Loans to risky borrowers and those with the longer maturities offer the highest yields. The safer and shorter loans usually yield significantly less than longer-term and riskier bonds. Bonds come in all kinds of shapes and sizes.

(Some quick definitions: Corporate bonds, of course, are loans to businesses. Junk bonds are high-yield [low- or un-rated] corporate bonds, which carry a higher interest rate in exchange for greater risk. Preferred stock pays fixed and generally higher dividends than common stock and also trades at a price that's usually more stable than common stock. Ginny Maes—or more properly, Government National Mortgage Association Pass-Through Certificates—are the highest-yielding government securities and provide mortgages for homebuyers. Series I bonds provide a fixed return and a supplemental return tied to inflation. And tax-free munis are, just as they sound, loans to state and local governments, the interest on which is not taxed by the federal government and not taxed by the state, either, if you live in the state where the bonds are issued.)

More management required

Most of these bonds, or bond-like instruments, can be bought singly or as part of a mutual fund. Many retirees prefer not to deal with individual bonds because:

• Trading individual bonds in small lots can get expensive.

- Small investors usually don't have access to the best bonds at the best prices.
- If individual bonds are redeemed or called before they mature, reinvestment decisions are required. That's something retirees may not want to deal with.

Thus, there is more management associated with purchasing individual bonds. Plus, there's always the potential risk of default, or the risk that a certain event could cause a rapid depreciation in a bond's value. (You may remember Dow Corning's breast-implant disaster, Johnson & Johnson's Tylenol scare, Orange County's [California] default, or other situations that affected the value of some individual bonds.) U.S. government bonds are, as a practical matter, not subject to default.

The advantages of bond funds include:

- Professional management and diversification.
- Bond fund managers usually can purchase the best bonds at the best prices due to the fund's size, economies of scale, and their research capabilities.
- Even if one or two bonds in a bond mutual fund run into problems, the yield and price of the overall bond fund will only be marginally affected. So the investor needn't worry about default risk having a substantial negative impact on most bond funds.

Several flavors

Bond mutual funds come in several flavors. Open-ended funds, closed-ended, and unit investment trusts (UITs) are the most common. (Open-ended means these funds offer an unlimited number of shares forever. Thus, you can redeem your shares with the mutual-fund company when you want the money. A closed-end fund sells only a certain number of shares. Thus, its shareholders must negotiate with other investors to sell their shares, which means the price received can be—and usually is—less than the quoted market price. UITs are groupings of bonds that are selected for similar maturity dates and interest rates, then held until maturity. When a given bond in the UIT matures, your pro-rata share of the proceeds is returned to you.)

Open-ended bond mutual funds are excellent in terms of providing consistent, competitive returns, but they do have one drawback. When you buy an individual bond, you know exactly when the bond matures. Therefore, you have little downside risk if you hold the bond until maturity.

But when you buy an open-ended bond fund, there is no definite date of maturity. There is an *average* maturity of the bonds in the portfolio, but no date when all bonds are paid off and all capital returned. In fact, if the average maturity on a bond fund is 20 years, it is conceivable that 10 years from now, it will still have a 20-year average maturity.

That's because as one bond matures, a new usually longer-term bond is purchased. That's also why the interest-rate risk in open-ended bond mutual funds must be understood before investing. Bond funds pay interest based on the underlying loans made. The yield will change slightly as some bonds mature and the fund manager takes the cash and buys a new bond at the current market rate. These changes in yield are gradual and hardly noticeable but can over time dramatically affect your income.

What does change is the principal value of the bond fund. If interest rates rise, the value of the bond fund declines. If interest rates decline, the value of the bond fund increases. This is a good reason for sharp Bucketeers to use GICs when rates are low and use mid- to longer-term bonds or a "hybrid" when rates are high. This maximizes the performance of Bucket No. 2 while minimizing the risk.

Don't chase yield

There are dozens of different bond funds to consider as a Bucket No. 2 asset. A word of caution: Do *not* get lured into buying those with the highest yields. Chasing yield or a hot fund in any investment is usually a recipe for disaster. Higher yields may also mean higher risk, so be careful.

While Bucket No. 2 can tolerate some volatility, it would be a mistake to invest all of it in, say, foreign bonds yielding 16% only to find out that by the time the foreign currency was converted into dollars, you actually lost 30%. Suitable bond investments for Bucket No. 2 would be solid, well-managed bond mutual funds. This could include high yield "junk" and even growth-and-income funds, preferred stock, or a portfolio of several different income-oriented funds. But to stay on the safe side, it's always better to allocate the greatest percentage of your income portfolio to high-quality corporate bonds, government bonds, and Ginnie Maes.

Other bond-type products

The sheer number and variety of bonds, bond funds, and Bucket No. 2-type assets can be confusing. So here's a quick rundown on some of the major kinds. (All of these—and in fact, all of the investments mentioned in this and the preceding chapter—are summarized in a chart at the end of this chapter.)

Growth and income funds split the assets between stocks and bonds. They often make more money in good times and lose more in bad times than their cousin, the *balanced fund* (which invests in all four asset classes—cash, government securities, corporate bonds, and stocks.) By contrast, an *equity income fund* invests just in stocks that pay dividends.

Intermediate- and long-term government securities are the best way to avoid default risks. These securities include Treasury notes, which mature in two to 10 years and Treasury bonds, which mature in 30 years. There are also U.S. Savings Bonds (Series EE), which you must hold at least six months; Series I (inflation-indexed) bonds, and TIPS (Treasury Inflation-Protected Securities). These all are subject to federal tax only (exempt from state tax) and, of course, are guaranteed by the federal government. The interest rates offered by all these are similar but are constantly changing. These securities are available individually or in funds.

Zero coupon bonds. With a zero, you don't receive interest every year. Instead, you buy them at a discount to their final maturity value. You know exactly what your return will be between now and the bond's maturity date. And unlike most bonds, zeros can't be called early, and there's no default risk. U.S. Savings Bonds, for example, are really zero coupons.

But the downsides are that you still pay taxes on the imputed (accrued but not received) income, so holding zeros in a tax-free account may be best. Because you don't get any interest payments, there are no decisions about reinvesting the interest.

Zeros are volatile and react wildly to interest-rate changes, but if you hold them to maturity, you know exactly what you will earn. That fact can be very comforting to nervous investors as long as they focus on the final maturity and ignore the ups and downs along the way. Zeros also are available individually or in funds.

Strategic-income funds. These funds seek high current income through a diversified portfolio made up largely of U.S. and foreign corporate bonds and government securities. They are "strategic" in that they're intended to help investors with long-term goals, such as college funding and retirement planning.

Foreign bond funds, naturally, hold bonds issued by other countries. But they are subject to the same foreign currency risk as international stocks. *Utility bond funds* invest in bonds issued by public utilities. These are relatively stable in price.

Variable annuities

These investments act a lot like tax-deferred mutual funds, but with a guarantee you won't lose principal if you die. (The insurance company pays to your heirs the full amount invested if you die, even if the market suffered a decline.) The name *variable* comes from the fact that the return varies with the performance of the "sub-accounts" you choose. If you invest in stock sub-accounts, your return will reflect the stock market's performance. Similarly, a bond sub-account will mirror the bond market. The money grows tax-deferred, so you don't pay taxes on your earnings until you withdraw the money.

There are many different kinds of variable annuities. Some are very competitive for either Bucket No. 2 or investing in Bucket No. 3. The ones I think most appropriate for Bucket No. 2 are those that give you a guaranteed rate of return of, say, 5% or 6%, *or* the return of the stock market portfolio held in the annuity for a specified number of years. You do pay an extra fee for this type of guarantee, and you may be forced to annuitize your guaranteed return over several years if you elect the fixed return. But during periods when stocks are producing dismal returns, your Bucket No. 2 will remain safe and earn at a reasonable rate. On the other hand, when stocks produce better returns, you get the greater of the two. Thus, if stocks go up, you get the returns of the stock market, and if stocks decline in value, you are protected with a guaranteed floor rate.

The downsides to variable annuities are that your money is locked up and also is subject to a surrender charge, management fees and mortality and expense charges. Sometimes these fees can be high (although there are many variable annuities with significantly lower fees) or with benefits well worth the fees you pay. Also, your money is subject to pre-age-59½ penalties, so you don't want a variable if you plan on touching the money before that magic age. Further, when you pull money out of a variable annuity, the earnings are taxed as ordinary income even if most of the gains came from capital appreciation. Once again in Bucket No. 2 this is O.K. because you will be spending this money.

Though an insurance product, variable annuities are really just another way to buy investments on a tax-deferred basis. They work particularly well if you are in a high tax bracket during your accumulation of assets and a lower tax bracket when you begin taking distributions. In fact, one recent study by the Big 5 CPA firm Price Water-house Coopers ("Variable Annuities and Mutual Fund Investments for Retirement Planning: A Statistical Comparison") concluded that variable annuities will outperform the identical returns of mutual funds long term, given a high tax bracket before retirement and a lower bracket postretirement. This is true even after the added costs of mortality and expense charges.

So if you happen to be in this situation, a variable annuity may be perfect for Bucket No. 3. However, you should also consider tax-managed equity portfolios and real estate. I'll cover those later.

Variable annuities are like an individual retirement account in that any withdrawals prior to age 59½ are subject to a 10% IRS penalty. Annuities do not enjoy a stepped-up tax basis at death, although many companies are adding tax-free death benefits to make annuities even more attractive.

Just as there are good and bad mutual funds and good and bad advisors, there are good and bad annuities. A well-trained financial planner can help you decide whether a variable annuity will work for you, and if so, which one. But as previously stated, these are complex investments that are constantly changing. They are definitely getting better and well worth looking into. You'll need to do your homework here, but don't throw the baby out with the bath water just because you may have heard insurance firms are ogres or variable annuities are bad. Sometimes they are a perfect fit, and sometimes they don't fit at all.

So as you can see, there are a lot of different ways to play the bond or quasi-bond game for Bucket No. 2. Here's an overall look at the advantages and disadvantages of bond-type products:

Pros:
- Pay fixed income.
- Return principal.
- Diversification and professional management easily attained in a bond fund.
- Potentially higher returns and a possibility of a floor with variable annuities.

Cons:
- Interest-rate risk to principal.
- Active management required by holders of individual bonds.
- Some default risk with non-government bonds.

What makes the entire *Buckets of Money*® strategy work so beautifully is that Bucket No. 1 buys you time to be a little more aggressive with Bucket No. 2, and Bucket No. 2 buys you time to go for the growth in Bucket No. 3.

But I know that the names and descriptions of some of these investments can be confusing. So the following chart lists all the options we've talked about so far and rates them on a scale of 1-to-5 as to their risk, return, liquidity, and tax efficiency and indicates for which bucket they are most appropriate. (Just to be clear, a "1" means *lowest* risk/yield/liquidity/tax break/ and total return while, of course, a "5" means *highest*.)

BEST BETS FOR BUCKETS NO. 1 AND 2

	Risk	Yield	Liquidity	Tax Break	Total Return
Certificate of Deposit (Buckets 1 & 2)	1	3	4	1	3
Immediate Annuities/GICs (Bucket 1)	1	2	1	3	3
Tax-Deferred Fixed Annuities/GICs (Bucket 2)	1	4	3	4	4
Intermediate- & Long-Term Gov't Securities (Bucket 2)	3	3	3	2	4
Tax-Free Municipal Bonds (Bucket 2)	3	3	3	5	2
GNMAs/Mortgage Bonds (Bucket 2)	3	4	3	2	4
Zero-Coupon Bonds (Bucket 2)	4	3	2	2	3

	Risk	Yield	Liquidity	Tax Break	Total Return
Preferred Stock (Bucket 2)	4	4	3	1	4
Series I Bonds (Bucket 2)	1	3	3	2	3
Closed End Bond Fund (Bucket 2)	3	4	3	1	3
Short-Term Bond Fund (Bucket 1)	2	2	4	1	2
Mid- or Long-term Bond Fund (Bucket 1 or 2)	4	3	4	1	3
High-Yield "Junk" Bonds (Bucket 2)	5	5	3	1	4
Strategic Income Funds (Bucket 2)	4	5	3	1	4
Foreign Bond Funds (Bucket 2)	5	5	2	1	4
Growth & Income Funds (Bucket 2)	4	5	3	3	5
Utility Funds (Bucket 2)	4	5	3	3	4
Equity Income Funds (Bucket 2)	5	5	3	3	5
Balanced Funds (Bucket 2)	4	5	3	3	5

(continued)

	Risk	Yield	Liquidity	Tax Break	Total Return
Variable Annuities (stock accounts) (Bucket 3 only unless with guaranteed floor)	4	5	2	4	4
Variable Annuities (bond accounts) (Bucket 2)	3	3	1	4	2

Chapter 7

THE THIRD BUCKET: INVESTING FOR LONG-TERM GROWTH

Congratulations! You've made it to Bucket No. 3, where you have a chance to see some *real* growth in your nest-egg, provided, of course, you think long-term and you think diversification.

The ultra-safe Bucket No. 1 will provide you income. The pretty-safe Bucket No. 2 will churn out yet more inflation-indexed income with which to replenish the first bucket. And the riskier Bucket No. 3—reserved for stocks and other long-term investments—aims for long-term appreciation.

Once you set up Bucket No. 3, you're going to enjoy a liberation. Why? Because unlike most stock-market investors, you're going to be firmly focused on the long-term (14 years in our example, but you could choose, say, 10 years or eight years if you're a very aggressive investor).

The key to successful stock-market investing, you'll remember from Chapter 1, is not when you invest or even which stocks you buy—but for *how long* you invest and *how diversified* you are. Given a long-enough time frame and proper diversification, this Bucket No. 3 ought to be where you get the biggest bang for your investment buck.

What is a stock?

If a bond, as we said in the last chapter, amounts to a loan by an investor to a firm or to a government, a share of stock represents ownership. You, the investor, own a very small portion of the company—or have *equity*—in it. Whereas with a bond you expect to get your money back, plus interest, you don't know with equities how much, if anything, you're going to receive when you sell.

So that's a risk: You may get back less than what you paid for the stock. But many investors are willing to take that risk because the long-term trend—if you own stocks in good companies—has been upward. Further, even if all your stocks don't do well, the most you can lose is 100% of your investment. But your potential gains (unlike those with bonds) are potentially unlimited.

More specifically, advantages to investing in the stock market include:

- *Stocks appreciate.* That is, they can grow in value. A company that does well, or is widely expected to do well, may see its share price rise.

- *Some stocks pay dividends.* This is akin to the interest paid by bonds, though neither as high nor as predictable. Average dividend yield is now less than 2%. That's not a lot, but if reinvested back into stocks, it will spur your portfolio's growth.
- *Stocks are tax-favored.* Interest—from bonds, CDs, bank accounts, and so on—is taxed as ordinary income as are stock dividends. But when you sell a stock that's gone up in value, your profit is taxed as a *capital gain.* And especially if you've owned the stock for more than a year, that capital gain is taxed at what's likely a significantly lower rate than ordinary income. (And holding for five years creates a new, super long-term capital-gains tax rate topping out at 18% and going as low as 8%, depending on your tax bracket.) What's more, you pay no capital gains taxes *until* you sell. And when you die, the capital gains that have accrued in your stocks pass onto your heirs tax-free.
- *Stocks are a hedge against inflation.* Stocks historically have grown more quickly than inflation. This is very important for our long-term bucket, Bucket No. 3.

(Incidentally, I'm going to give you a lot of investing basics in this book. But if you want to explore that general topic further, I heartily recommend Jordan Goodman's books, especially *Everyone's Money Book* and his book of financial definitions. He clearly and fully tells how to maximize returns on cash, pick individual stocks, select mutual funds, invest in bonds and real estate, and much more that's helpful to the individual investor. His books—and other such reading recommendations—are listed in Appendix A.)

The core of the Buckets philosophy, of course, is letting that third bucket grow. While you spend safe money from Bucket No. 1 and accumulate semi-safe money in Bucket No. 2, you can leave your Bucket No. 3 alone for a number of years. This was particularly important during our most recent bear market, which began in March 2000 and was further complicated by the financial trauma caused by terrorism.

With a 12- to 14-year time horizon for Bucket No. 3, even a grizzly bear shouldn't cause you too much concern. By being a long-term investor you can blissfully ignore the "BUY THIS STOCK NOW!" headlines that leap out at you from newspapers and magazines. You can just smile when your pal at work suggests a "can't miss" stock. You can cleanse your mind of all the gloomy talk about a looming recession or the hopeful chatter about a possible boom. No more biting your fingernails and debating, "Should I get in? What if it hasn't bottomed yet?" Or "Should I sell? What if it hasn't peaked yet."

You won't care. You will have parked a big chunk of your money in Bucket No. 3 and will leave it there for years.

The key, of course, is getting it parked in the right places and in the right amounts and having a knowledgeable person keep an eye on it. There's no way around it, that takes expertise. All but the most sophisticated investors are going to need help.

You're going to want to pick an able financial advisor. Why? Because the truth is, by the time important financial information—e.g., a certain mutual fund manager is buying value stocks even though the fund is nominally oriented to growth—gets to the general public, it's too late. You need an advisor whose antenna is finely attuned to such changes. It may help if he/she has been around for a while and is a Certified Financial Planner (CFP™), a Chartered Financial Analyst (CFA), a Chartered Financial Consultant (ChFC), or a Chartered Life Underwriter (CLU) and registered as an investment advisor. (It's O.K. if the advisor isn't designated quite yet as long as he or she is working toward a designation or is teamed up with someone who is designated.) But it takes more than a designation to be a good advisor. It takes some brains, some experience, some strategy, and *a lot* of integrity.

Really good advisors are hard to come by. When you find one—somebody who cares more about your financial well-being than his own—then you'll be able to sleep well at night knowing your portfolio is diverse and its volatility will be held to a minimum.

Because picking such a person or team is so important, Chapter 10 will go into great detail about how to find such an advisor. Meanwhile, let's look at some of the issues and the nomenclature you should first be familiar with so you can work with your advisor to best tailor a Bucket No. 3 for you.

Individual stocks vs. mutual funds

As you know, owning many stocks is safer than having just one or just a few. Understand, though, that owning a portfolio of stocks, rather than a few, reduces the likelihood that you're going to get rich quick. But getting rich quick is *not* what we're trying to do; we're just trying to get rich over the long haul. Or, as I like to say . . .

Lucia's Law | **21**

Stock-market investing isn't about achieving perfection. You need good—but not spectacular—results to do well long-term.

So how do you diversify the stocks in your Bucket No. 3? Well, you can buy stocks of a bunch of individual companies. But I don't recommend that.

Doing the necessary research is very tedious. And, statistically and psychologically, it's an uphill slog: You're not likely to do as well with individual stocks. Equally important, if you go the individual-stock route, you've still got to deal with the emotion of picking them and figuring out when to sell them and learning to ignore tips from friends and emails from stock-touting sharpies who say they have an inside track on a hot deal.

Life is simpler—and likely more profitable—if you forget about individual stocks for Bucket No. 3 and instead stick with mutual funds. But if you *must*—if you crave the adrenaline or the sense of ownership or whatever it is that makes individual stocks ring your bell—then by all means use your financial advisor as a sounding board before you invest in those. Yes, you'll have to pay a commission to discuss your choices, but it'll be worth it. (And those commissions are negotiable.)

Most Bucketeers, though, would be far better off as mutual-fund investors. A mutual fund is an investment company that pools your money with that of thousands of other investors and employs a professional manager to buy various securities, of which you then own a fraction. The price of your mutual-fund shares (called the net asset value, or N.A.V.) rises or falls daily with the market value of the securities held by the fund.

The fund's profits (or losses) are distributed to the investors on a pro-rata basis. So putting your money in a mutual fund means you own a small piece of probably scores or even hundreds of individual stocks rather just a few . . . so it's instant diversification.

In addition to diversification and professional management, other benefits of mutual funds include: (1) the fund handles the paperwork; (2) it's easy to get information about a fund (most have toll-free 800-numbers); (3) it's easy (sometimes *too* easy) to switch money within fund families if your goals or the fund's performance change; (4) the fund usually keeps tabs on the tax situation.

The fund also automatically reinvests the dividends and capital gains. Which brings me to the next point: How do mutual funds make you money? While there is no guarantee your mutual fund will produce profits over the long run, most do. The profits come as the underlying value of the businesses (companies the fund owns stock in) appreciate in value. As the businesses become more successful, their stock increases in value—and the mutual fund value grows as well. So one way you, the mutual fund investor, can make money is by selling your shares at a profit. (But that's not something you're going to want to do soon in the life of Bucket No. 3; you're going to let those profits grow.)

Your mutual funds can also grow from your share of the dividends received quarterly from its pool of stocks and from capital gains distributions made once a year. Capital gains means the profits in excess of losses on the sales by the fund manager of securities in the portfolio. So although you may not be selling your fund shares, the manager will be selling and buying shares in various companies as he or she tries to best position the fund. Once a year the profit or loss (usually in December) from those transactions is split among the investors.

So, again, the two ways your fund shares can grow are through your dividends and through profitable transactions made by the fund manager on stocks that have appreciated. Understand, though, a mutual fund is not like a CD or bond that cranks out a preordained return. Even the best funds do not always grow each year. A bad year for the market in general may translate to a bad year for the fund's holdings. Or the market may have a good year, but the portion of the market targeted by your fund (*e.g.,* small-cap growth or large-cap value stocks) may be down. Or regardless of the market trend, the manager may just make poor decisions and end up with capital losses instead of capital gains.

So, with funds as with individual stocks, there is a risk, and there is no guarantee. But I believe if you properly diversify, rebalance, and invest for the long-term, you can minimize that risk.

How to select the right funds

Funds have lots of advantages. But they also have a staggering variety of objectives and philosophies. You're not really diversified if you have a bunch of funds that all own the same—or many of the same—stocks. You need funds that have different goals, different operating styles, and different managers.

For purposes of Bucket No. 3, you probably want what's generally classified as a "stock" mutual fund as opposed to one that invests in government securities, municipal bonds, foreign currencies, or the like. Because you're going to let this bucket grow for years, you aren't so worried about risk (which will diminish with time) or being tax-free (which will reduce your returns.) Getting *growth* is what's important for this bucket. Getting "tax-managed" growth is even better!

Yet with thousands of stock mutual funds to choose from (many with confusing names and equally opaque objectives), choosing the right ones takes a little time and effort. Here are some factors to look at as you compare funds:

N.A.V.: This is the fund's net-asset value, or what it costs to buy one share in the fund. This is derived by dividing the total value of all the fund's holdings by the number of the fund's outstanding shares. Tracking N.A.V. lets you know if the value of your investment in the fund is going up or down. You can find this figure in the newspaper or on the Internet every day.

Total return: This shows changes in the prices of the shares plus the results of investing the income/dividends as well as any capital gains or losses after expenses. This is the best figure to use (as opposed to yield, which is the amount the fund is paying to shareholders) when comparing one fund to another. The total return figures for 1-, 3-, and 5-years as well as from the beginning of the current year, can be found in financial publications or obtained through the fund directly. (Another excellent source is Morningstar, a weekly reference service that comprehensively tracks the record of all mutual funds. Its web site is www. morningstar.com)

Look at the total return over a long period that includes both bull and bear markets. You may find that some of the best funds never are No. 1 in any year but do better than the overall market in up years and lose less than the overall market in down years.

Fees. There are two kinds: sales fees and management fees. You will want to know if a fund is a "load" or "no load." (Load means it charges a sales commission.) There's no evidence that load funds perform better. In fact, as I often put it . . .

Lucia's Law | **22**

A load is a marketing cost, nothing more and nothing less. It won't make a bad fund perform better or a good one worse.

So it comes down to this: If you don't need help selecting a fund, you're probably better off saving the sales fee and choosing a no-load.

However, in a backhanded way, load funds may actually have an edge. That's because . . .

Lucia's Law | **23**

A load may help you do the right thing for the wrong reason: If it keeps you from jumping from fund to fund, it's worth the cost.

In other words, if having to pay a load effectively makes you into a buy-and-hold investor, hallelujah! Being a tightwad has made you do the right thing.

In addition to the load, every fund—load or no-load—charges a management fee. A typical fee is .5% to 1% or more. (Some higher-risk funds, like small cap or emerging international markets, may charge 1.5% to 2%. Those funds, if selected at all, should be added to your portfolio in small doses because they are very risky in addition to being costly.)

Turnover rate. This is the dollar amount of stocks sold by the fund manager relative to a fund's total assets. High turnover rates mean high commission costs and large capital-gains distributions, which in turn means higher taxes. Many well-run funds have turnover rates of 30%–50%. However, there are sometimes good reasons for high turnovers, such as the funds being "tax managed." Again, Morningstar and a good advisor can help explain a fund's turnover rate and whether it's reasonable.

Size. This tells you the amount of assets the fund manages. A fund that's too small may incur higher administrative costs. A good rule of thumb might be to avoid any fund that's stuck at the $50-million level or below for several years. If it hasn't grown, it may be because its lackluster performance has attracted few new investors.

Beta. This is a fund's volatility compared to market as a whole (with the market = 1.0). With a beta higher than 1.0, the fund fluctuates more than the market as a whole. With a beta below 1.0, just the opposite.

Manager. It's not a bad idea to look for a manager (or a group of managers) who have been with a fund—or at least, the fund family—for a few years. Non-performing managers tend not to last long. Morningstar also provides lots of information about managers.

How many funds should you own?

So if you—by yourself or with an advisor—find funds that look good, the question becomes: How many do you buy? There's no hard-and-fast rule about this. Common sense, though, plays a part. An accepted view is that seven or eight is probably as many as you can regularly track. I normally recommend a large-cap growth, large-cap value, small-cap growth, small-cap value, international, emerging markets, and real estate.

Remember, your aim is to cover a number of different aspects of the market with funds that will do well during different parts of the economic cycle. You want funds that don't all march to the same drummer. Some (financial-services stocks, for example) do better in periods of high growth and low interest rates while others (such as pharmaceutical stocks) may outperform during down times. You want to have all the bases covered.

How to get diversified

What makes Bucket No. 3 really work is broad diversification and a multi-asset/multi-style/multi-manager approach to investing the money. How do you get that kind of team of money managers working for you? Well, you're going to need to hire a financial advisor who is up to date on asset-allocation strategy and who can work with a money-manager selection firm to help pick good fund managers and continuously monitor their performance relative to risk. Your advisor will hold those managers to their style discipline (*e.g.,* growth, value, large-cap, small-cap . . . whatever.) And if your advisor is good, he or she won't be afraid to terminate those managers who consistently under-perform relative to their benchmarks.

I can't stress enough how critical it is that the money managers do not overlap in terms of their investment styles. If you have a large-growth manager, for example, who, when value stocks get hot, starts gravitating toward value in order to pump up his results, that's going to leave you under-invested in growth stocks. It's also going to set you up for a fall.

A classic case of this was in the year 2000 when tech stocks were riding high after several years of phenomenal gains. A lot of nominally non-tech managers lusted for some of those tech stocks to bolster their portfolios. (There's intense competition among managers to get quarterly results that'll make their fund stand out.) And folks with 401(k) plans started switching their holdings into large-cap tech.

Can you guess what happened? Well, around spring of 2000, tech took a bad tumble. Intel, Cisco, Dell Computer, Sun Microsystems, Microsoft—all good companies and all tremendous players over the past three or more years—got creamed. The tech-heavy NASDAQ index fell almost 40% in the calendar year 2000 and almost 70% from its March, 2000 high to its 2001 low.

In truth, the year 2000 was not a good one for stocks in general. But if you were in a value fund that had transformed itself into a tech-growth fund, you were really in trouble. Growth went south in a big way, but value more or less held its own and some types of value funds—small cap, for example—were up significantly. So if you thought you were in value but really were in growth, you got the worst of both worlds: What you thought you were in stayed even or went up but what you were really in fell like a rock. *Surprise!*

So it's important for managers to be style-specific and to have style discipline. I like to see investors use an investment advisory team with multiple managers, each operating in a different style. As long as the managers aren't buying the same stocks and stick with their disciplines and are measured against reliable benchmarks, then you can get an accurate reading as to how they're performing.

Judging performance, again, takes a seasoned eye. For example, if your portfolio grew by 28% in a year, that would sound pretty good, right? Generally, yes. But a few years ago, a large growth portfolio should have brought in about 38% and thus, a 28% return would have been under-performing. By contrast, a large value portfolio that did 12% that year when the S&P did 28% might look anemic. But actually, 12% might have put you 20%–30% above what other large value managers were earning. So it's critical to understand which benchmark you're using as an evaluation tool. And then you and your advisor can hold your money managers to that mark.

What does your pie chart look like?

Your financial advisor will help you figure out what mix of funds is right for your Bucket No. 3. Your risk tolerance, how you feel about the market's future, and other factors are taken into account.

A classic, all-growth portfolio might look like Chart 7-1:

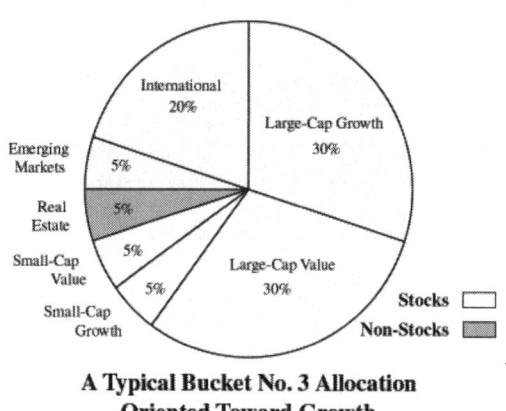

A Typical Bucket No. 3 Allocation
Oriented Toward Growth
Chart 7-1

What the advisor will try to do is to find asset classes that don't move in lockstep with one another. For example, tech stocks (which are generally in the large growth category) might have been down almost 40% in the year 2000, but the average growth mutual fund was down only about 6%. So even though they both were down, the combination of the two still would have given you a much better portfolio than if you had just one.

Lump-sum investing or dollar-cost averaging?

You read a lot in the popular financial press about the joys of dollar-cost averaging (DCA). That's where money is invested in increments over a long period rather than as a lump sum. There are times when DCA makes perfect sense. When you're automatically putting a part of your paycheck into your 401(k) plan at work or adding to your IRA, you are dollar-cost averaging. And that's fine.

But that's usually not the way to invest your Bucket No. 3. For me, using DCA for that task is too much like trying to time the market, and you know what I think about that.

In fact, consider this . . .

Lucia's Law — **24**

Dollar-cost averaging is like a little voice saying, "I'm so afraid of this market that I'll just invest in dribs and drabs." Long-term investors needn't have that fear.

The average bull market runs almost 40 months, and the average bear market about 19 months. Thus, roughly every third or fourth year, stocks have a down year. But that means three out of four are up years. If you dollar-cost average in an up market, you're going to have a lot of money sitting on the sidelines before you're fully invested. So you're going to miss out on a lot of potential return, and to me that's foolish.

What I recommend instead is asset allocation. Don't try to pick a good time to jump into the market or try to invest a little bit in both good times and bad. Instead, asset allocation means using your head (and your advisor's know-how) to set up the best possible model—and then allow this diversification to smooth out the market's ride as much as possible.

I repeat: There are *no* guarantees. But if you have a multi-asset, multi-style, multi-manager approach, there's not a whole lot that can upset your apple cart over the long-run. If the market goes up, you're going to go up. If the market goes down, you're going to go down—but you're not going to get walloped the way someone will who tried and failed to time the market.

Judging performance

How do you and your advisor decide if a manager is doing a good job? The truth is, the markets continually fluctuate, sectors soar and fall, and styles of investing ebb and flow. You don't want to cut somebody off at the knees because, say, he's a large-tech fund manager and the year 2000 was a lousy one for large tech stocks. Or even if large-tech had an O.K. year but this particular manager did not. But if he *consistently* fails to meet his benchmark, then he's gotta go. Let's face it: He's a lousy stock picker.

So you're going to need some help in figuring out if the fund managers are performing well. Are they running the fund according to its stated objectives and not chasing after the latest "hot" equities? Are they meeting their benchmarks, which usually means one of the accepted indexes, such as the Dow Jones (for big firms), the Russell 2000 (for small-cap stocks), the Standard & Poors 500 or the Wilshire 5000 (for the broad market).

And, in addition, if yours is a taxable portfolio, is the manager doing the best for you tax-wise? If not, you're giving up real money, real rate of return, that you don't need to.

I'll talk some more about some of these issues in the next chapter, but the point is that everybody's situation is unique. To make the very best use of your Bucket No 3, you're going to need help. And to coin a phrase, you get what you pay for. If you hire a really sharp and talented financial advisor who understands the architecture of your financial plan, that will compensate for a lot of things, even under-performance. For instance, if one portfolio produces a 10% return but gives back 2½% in taxes while another, more tax-efficient fund produces a 9% return, which would you prefer?

Kinds of stock investments

Even if you have a good advisor, you still will want to become a knowledgeable investor who understands something about the markets and can have a dialogue with your team. So it's to your advantage to learn what you can about the kinds of stock investments an advisor might choose for you. Let's look at some of these vehicles and how they might help or deter your Bucket No. 3:

Balanced funds. Most mutual funds invest in just one asset class, say, stocks. But a balanced fund puts a portion of its assets into each of the four major asset classes: stocks, bonds, government securities, and cash. It sounds good in theory—like instant diversification. But to me they're akin to market-timing funds. The idea is that the manager will bulk up on bonds or stocks, depending on where he/she thinks the market is going. But, in truth, nobody knows. Even if you're the smartest person in America, you don't know what the market is going to do. So it's much better to design a good diversified model than try to predict highs and lows.

Growth and income funds. Similarly, these funds split the assets between stocks and bonds. But the problem is much the same as with the balanced fund—the manager is tempted to "bet" on which sector is likely to be on the rise. However, some growth and income funds invest largely in income-producing stocks that pay dividends. These may be quite adequate for the value portion of the portfolio.

Sector funds. These buy stocks of only one industry— energy, perhaps. Or telecommunications, airlines, retailers, or just about any field you can think of. But such sectors can ricochet wildly, so these are very speculative. Sector funds should be an option only if an investor has money to burn and wants to "play" the market with a small amount of his portfolio, say 5%.

If you're hooked on daring challenges and can afford to lose the money, go right ahead. But it's a gamble, like putting 5% in gold. Most of us are better off allowing a professional money manager make the decisions on which sectors to include, for instance, in a large-cap growth fund.

Now something quite interesting happens when you combine a group of sector funds—say, 5% in telecom, 5% in health care, 5% in financial services, and 5% in natural resources. Together, they may make up a large-cap growth fund on steroids. But this type of strategy is not for the fainthearted and needs the careful attention of a qualified advisor.

Index funds. These attempt to duplicate the performance of a market index by buying the same stocks that compose the index, whether it be, for example, the Dow Jones Industrial Average, the NASDAQ Composite, the NASDAQ 100, the Standard & Poors 500, or whatever. These could make a lot of sense for the Bucket No. 3 investor, especially in a taxable account.

Index funds are effectively unmanaged funds because the fund buys the stocks in a particular index and then just holds them. Since most indexes are market-capitalization weighted, most of your money goes into the largest 50 companies of, say, the S&P 500. Thus when the market is going down, you're investing more money in those big companies. Likewise, when the market is soaring, you are placing your money in the most expensive stocks. Among the advantages of index funds are that they have low turnover and thus are fairly tax efficient.

In recent years, managers who actively traded have had trouble beating the indexes. The S&P 500, for example, is mostly weighted toward growth stocks. Thus, value managers are not going to beat that index when growth stocks are hot as they were in the late '90s.

So I sometimes recommend index funds for efficient markets like the Dow, S&P, and to a much lesser extent, NASDAQ. But for investing in less efficient markets like international stocks, small caps, emerging markets and the like, I think you'd be better off to have a money manager picking the stocks and being geared to pulling the trigger when and if the trigger needs to be pulled.

As you can tell, I'm foursquare in favor of actively managed accounts. That way it's easier to assess the risk in the portfolio—in other words, to try to get index returns, or better, with lower-than-index risk.

Maybe the best of all worlds is to have your portfolio part-managed and part-indexed. (The indexed part would be the large growth and value portion of your personal account and would give you some tax efficiency; the managed part would be for your IRA or 401(k). You can invest in bonds, REITs, and other taxable-type investments because taxes are not an issue inside a tax-sheltered plan. You can also use active management for the less efficient markets like small caps and international funds where stock-picking is paramount.) That way, when indexing is in favor and momentum is driving the market up, you have the advantage. And when active managers are in the driver's seat, you're still O.K.

You can also buy certain stocks that track the performance of an index. These are called *exchange-traded funds,* or ETFs. They trade just like any other stock but will perform very near the index they track. You can buy these stocks, unlike mutual funds, throughout the trading day rather than getting the price at the close of the trading session. So more active traders prefer ETFs over funds. Frankly, I don't care one way or the other.

Just a few, quick words on some other types of stock funds:

Large Capitalization funds (or Large Cap) buy stocks of big companies worth a lot of money. General Electric and General Motors, for example, are unlikely to go broke. Thus, these funds are safer than some, though their size also makes them less likely to spurt upward.

Small Cap funds. You guessed it! These are funds of smaller companies that have a greater risk of going belly-up but also more potential for quantum increases in profit.

Equity income funds. These, also known as Dividend Yield funds, buy stocks that pay dividends, meaning usually larger, established companies.

Global funds. These funds buy stocks from nations around the globe, including the United States.

International funds. Ditto . . . except these exclude any U.S. stocks, thus helping you to diversify if you already own funds holding American companies.

There are many more kinds of stock mutual funds. But those are some of the obvious categories you may run into when huddling with your financial advisor. One other distinction you might want to be alert to: the difference between *open-* and *closed-end* funds. Most funds are open-end, meaning they offer an unlimited number of shares forever and thus you can sell back your shares (known as *redeeming* them) to the mutual fund company when you want to take your money out.

By contrast, a closed-end fund sells only a certain number of shares. When you want to sell, you can't redeem them with the company and instead must find buyers on the New York Stock Exchange. Thus, the sale price isn't the N.A.V. but whatever you can negotiate, which usually means something less than the N.A.V.

A buyer may think he or she is getting them cheaply, but in truth closed-end shares hardly ever rise to their

N.A.V., so they're not likely to be much of a bargain. Every so often a closed-end fund sells at a substantial discount to its N.A.V., and there may be some good money to be made but that's usually not the case.

The bottom-line: Closed-end funds are widely misunderstood, so I don't do much with them. You probably shouldn't, either.

What about families of funds?

Many large mutual-fund companies have dozens or scores of funds covering every aspect of the market—growth, value, different sectors, big cap, small cap, you name it. Which raises the question: Is there an advantage to keeping your funds within one fund family? The definitive answer: Yes and no.

At some fund families, they manage by committee. That is, all the managers share their favorite stocks, then all go out and buy roughly the same stocks for their portfolios. That defeats the purpose of diversification. When the market tide eventually turns against them (and it *will!*), they'll all need to sell. That means an awful lot of money will leave the family. Which, in turn, means more selling, which means yet more capital gains and higher taxes for you—and even worse, the possibility of lower returns.

For a small investor, sticking with one family may be a good idea. Especially if you paid a load. But for any Bucketeer with a hefty sum to put in his Bucket No. 3, the smart course would be to work with your advisor to find either a family that doesn't have a lot of overlap among its funds' holdings, or choose non-overlapping funds from various families.

The joys of re-balancing

The typical Bucket No. 3 investor doesn't need to worry about switching funds as much as he does about re-balancing. If your fund managers are meeting their benchmarks, you don't need to worry about changing funds. But you did need to think about re-balancing.

You may remember from the early chapters that re-balancing is when you periodically redistribute your money to keep consistent with your goals. This is especially important when markets fluctuate a lot as they did in the year 2000. Let's say you were supposed to have 30% of your portfolio invested in large growth. But large growth got killed in 2000, so your overall portfolio fell 8%, and 6% of that was attributable to the decline in large growth.

You look at your portfolio and see that your large growth has declined from 30% to 27% of the total. So you're under-weighted there and over-weighted in other categories. What do you do? You buy growth. You take some money from the categories that have done well, and you plop it into growth.

It's sort of like being on a hot streak in Las Vegas. Do you take your winnings and bet them all on the next roll of the dice or spin of the wheel? You *could* (and casino owners love those who do.) But a more prudent idea is to stick some of your gain into your pocket to fund next summer's vacation or make the next car payment.

That takes discipline. But in investing, discipline works. Re-balancing is far better than market timing because over the long haul you're forcing yourself to sell high and buy low. You sell the good stuff and buy the ugly stuff, and it usually pays off.

Helping you re-balance is another task your advisor gets paid to do. You will need to set the criteria, such as how often (*e.g.,* monthly, quarterly, or yearly?) and how much of a differential will trigger a re-balancing (*e.g.,* when your percentages are off by 2%? By 3%?). Further, you'll need to give him or her guidelines as to whether to re-balance just retirement accounts (in which taxes on sales are deferred) or all accounts and how much cost is acceptable to execute this buying and selling.

Investment fads to avoid

But whatever you do, avoid fad investing. Among the dubious, fad-like ideas are:

> *"Dogs of the Dow."* This is a concept in which investors buy the poorest performing of the Dow Jones Industrial Average stocks each year. It's based on the idea that stocks with the highest dividend yield are most likely to rise in price. Unfortunately, it is a bad idea.
>
> It may work in some years when value stocks are in favor. But as a long-term investing philosophy, forget it. Ditto for several variations, such as the "Small

Dogs" theory, in which you invest in, say, the five lowest-priced of the 10 highest-yielding Dow stocks.

DRIPs. This is an acronym for Direct (or Dividend) Reinvestment Plans. It's one of those concepts that sounds good on the surface because it allows the small investor to avoid brokerage commissions and buy fractional shares while dollar-cost averaging. But in truth, it's a nightmare of accounting. Tax-wise, DRIPs are so complicated you practically need to hire a Big 5 accounting firm to figure out the cost basis of your shares. I think DRIPS in a personal account are a waste of time. If you must buy them, please do so in your IRA.

What's more, the rise and sophistication of mutual funds has made DRIPs an idea whose time has come *and* gone. If you can buy a mutual fund for $25 a month and in so doing, get diversification, professional management, and precise tax accounting, why would you want to bother with DRIPS? Beats me. I think DRIPS are a waste of time.

Buying on splits. What's better, two nickels or a dime? That's the question at the heart of buying on splits. The answer, of course, is: It doesn't matter. A split occurs when a company's board of directors changes (usually increases) the number of outstanding shares. If you had 100 shares and the stock split 2-for-1, you'd have 200 shares, but each would be worth only half as much and pay half the dividends. So what have you gained? It's true that firms that split tend to be confident about their future and thus, their stock may be on the rise. But if so, it's probably going to be on the rise whether the stock splits or not, and the spurt in price that sometimes follows a stock-split announcement may be temporary. Instead of watching splits, watch the company's fundamentals. If you're investing for the long term, you want a firm that has strong enough revenue, earnings, and dividend growth to keep on track, with or without a split.

Rolling stocks. This involves figuring out which stocks move in a predictable pattern, then buying at the low end of the range and selling at the high end . . . and doing it over and over again. The trouble, of course, lies with the word *predictable.* This is a short-term strategy that may work for a while on some stocks. But sooner or later either that stock or the market as a whole will throw you a curve. Again, it's better to invest for the long term and in companies with real potential rather than those that may or may not be predictably cyclical.

Non-stock holdings for Bucket No. 3

Stocks should be the primary vehicle in your Bucket No. 3. But there may be room for other long-term investments as well, principally real estate.

Like stocks, real estate over the long term can grow in value and produce income. And it's usually not as volatile as stocks because it takes a lot longer to buy or sell than just calling up your mutual-fund company or financial advisor. So there's less day-to-day fluctuation in prices, and that's good. But on the other hand, this lack of liquidity also means you can get stuck with an unsalable piece of property on which you're paying a mortgage, taxes, and upkeep, and that's not so great.

So real estate, while worth considering for Bucket No. 3, brings its own baggage. I think real estate is better as a Bucket No. 3 complement to stocks rather than as a replacement for. In the next chapter, I'll talk about some situations where real-estate might be a good way to go.

Of course, there are different ways to own real estate. Let's look at some of those:

Income property. Keep in mind that buying rental property usually requires a large initial cash outlay as well as what's often lots of management hassles for you, the landlord. Ideally, if you go the real-estate route for Bucket No. 3, you ought to be diversified there, too, meaning multiple properties—and that can really get costly.

Owner-occupied real estate. Most people already have a fair amount of real estate if one considers the family home. Is that a Bucket No. 3 investment? It *could* be, but probably you shouldn't look at it that way. After all, unlike your stocks and income property, you can't exactly sell it and live off it in retirement—you'll still need a place to live. So the fact that your home appreciated may not mean too much if when you sell it, you have to buy another, equally expensive home.

If the value of your home rises significantly and there's a way to tap into that equity by selling and, thus, help fund your retirement, great! This works well when you sell a really expensive home and move to an area where houses are cheaper. Since married couples can exclude up to $500,000 of capital gains on their principal residence (up to $250,000 for single people), this could be a nifty way to get extra income at retirement.

But it's best not to count on your home as part of your Bucket No. 3. If your home turns out to be a great investment, that's a bonus. But if it doesn't, you've still planned well and will be O.K. And, understand, the house may not work out as an investment because it (1) may not rise in value (2) may rise but you may not be able to sell it for what it's worth when you want to and (3) you may need to buy another one, which could end up costing you as much, or more.

The best plan, then, is to just live in your house and enjoy it. If it turns out to help your retirement, that's a windfall . . . but not something you're counting on.

Limited partnerships. There are LPs for oil and gas exploration, motion pictures, and even Broadway plays as well as for real estate. These were big a decade or so ago, though changes in tax laws have reduced their allure somewhat. The basic idea is that instead of buying property on your own, you pool your funds with other investors (the limited partners) and give the money to a manager (the general partner) who buys, operates, and eventually sells the property at a profit, which is then split proportionally among the investors.

Such partnerships got a bad name in the 1980s because some general partners took advantage of the investors. But if you've got a trustworthy general partner and if there are strong economics to the deal (as opposed to just the lure of tax write-offs), it makes some sense for small investors to join forces to buy larger and potentially more profitable pieces of property than they could afford individually. Going in with 30 other investors to buy a $3-million apartment house, say, can be much better for your Bucket No. 3 than buying a $300,000 duplex and having to personally manage it.

But *be careful!* The potential for abuse always exists because the limited partner has no way of controlling what goes on at the general-partner level until it's too late. Then the only option is to sue, and that's a losing game for the investor.

REITs. Real-Estate Investment Trusts are somewhat akin to partnerships, except their shares trade on the stock market. Thus, REIT investors, unlike those in limited partnerships, can sell whenever they wish. So this is a very liquid kind of real-estate investment.

But that's both good news and bad. REIT shares wax and wane, just like any other stock. So buying REITs does give you real estate and may produce a fine income stream, but it doesn't shield you from the market's volatility.

REITs do provide excellent diversification in a Bucket No. 3 portfolio. Studies show a 20% REIT allocation in a balanced portfolio increased the return over time and decreased the volatility.

There are many different types of REITs, such as those that hold residential, commercial, or health-care properties. Each requires due diligence before investing, but they may be suitable as part of Bucket No. 3 while at the same time producing income to reduce the amount of capital needed to invest in Bucket No. 1.

Another possibility: Variable life

In the previous chapter, I talked about the pros and cons of variable annuities as a Bucket No. 2 or Bucket No. 3 investment. The upsides include having an insurance company select the fund managers for the sub accounts, the investments are tax deferred until the money is withdrawn, you can rebalance your portfolio or use an automatic rebalancing feature, and you can receive a guaranteed death benefit if you die shortly after a market decline. The downsides are surrender charges, mortality expenses, and no step-up basis upon death.

Variable life insurance also comes with surrender charges and mortality charges, but its tax treatment makes it a very attractive long-term investment for those in high tax brackets who also need life insurance. Variable universal life provides a tax-free death benefit, tax-free withdrawals of your premiums, and the ability to borrow your earnings tax free to help supplement your retirement income. There's no pre-age-59½ penalty problem, and due to its tax-free death benefit, any loan is paid off when the insured dies.

While life insurance is not intended to be a Bucket No. 3 investment, many times it is the best investment for those not needing to spend all of the money in Bucket No. 3 and wanting to pass on the highest after-tax inheritance. However, variable universal life may not be appropriate for those in lower tax brackets with high needs for temporary death benefits. Term life is much better to fill that need. But in certain cases a properly funded variable life policy can be a great supplement to your 401(k), Roth IRA, 529 plan, and tax-deferred and education IRAs.

Other non-stock, non-real estate investments

Some folks like to go beyond stocks and real estate in search of other long-term assets that *may* appreciate in their Bucket No. 3. I'm dubious. Too often this means they invest in something they really like, such as old movie posters or Cabbage Patch dolls. And it's fine that they enjoy those, and even better if the items increase in value over the years.

But an investor's fondness for the objects can obscure reason and good judgment. Besides, stocks or real estate have proven track records as growth vehicles. So they are much safer places to put your retirement savings.

> *Collectibles.* This means things like coins, gems, stamps, art, antiques, vintage wines, or comic books. The value of these ebb and flow in public favor. I don't like them as investments. I think collectibles are a hobby, not a true investment, and lack any semblance of predictability. At least with stocks, you know what the long-term trend is. I don't think there is any predictable trend with old cars or diamonds or baseball cards. If you really like old cars, diamonds, or baseball cards, great. Collect as many as you can afford, display them nicely, admire them lovingly, show them off to friends and family. And if they appreciate, you're ahead of the game. Just don't count on that appreciation—and don't consider it part of your Buckets.

> *Precious metals.* Every investment text ever written says that gold is a good inflation hedge. But we haven't had serious inflation in quite a while, and anybody who bought gold in the last 10 to 15 years has been sorely disappointed. Precious metals have been flat, or worse, since the late '70s, and my advice is to ignore the advice of the occasional doomsayer who tells you that gold and silver will save you in the event of a worldwide economic cataclysm.

Well, there is more that could be said about what to put in Bucket No. 3. And I'll give you some more examples in the next chapter.

But for now, keep in mind that:

- *You need to reserve Bucket No. 3 for long-term growth.* You almost never put money-market funds, say, or bonds in this bucket. Your best bet is stock mutual funds and perhaps some real-estate.
- *You will need a financial advisor.* He/she will help you get properly diversified and to keep tabs on the fund managers so that they stick to their objectives and meet their benchmarks.
- *You must re-balance your portfolio periodically.* Your advisor can do this, but you can and should set the criteria.

Chapter 8

GETTING YOUR BUCKETS ALL LINED UP

Now that you know what kinds of investments work best for each bucket, what do you do? How do you organize your buckets and when, if ever, do you change that setup?

One of the beauties of the Buckets system is that it's so flexible. I've often mentioned the example of the three main buckets and time frames of seven, seven, and 14 years, respectively. But there's nothing cut in stone about that. You might want to do five-year buckets or even, in effect, change the number of buckets. As you'll see in this chapter, it's quite possible and/or desirable—depending on individual circumstances—to vary the number of years or to make buckets within the buckets.

What's most important is that you have a personal investment strategy built around *you*—your goals, your time frame, and your tolerance for risk. In today's complex investment world, even expert investors find it hard to create and implement a well-structured investment plan on their own. So, again, I strongly urge you to work with investment professionals who understand your needs and can help you develop a prudent strategy that will both protect and grow your wealth.

But so you can better work with those professionals, let's look at some of the scenarios and principles you might encounter whether you are (1) a long way from retirement, (2) nearing retirement, or (3) already retired.

❑ **Pre-retirement.**

If you're well shy of retirement, you're in an enviable position. You've got many years, perhaps decades, to let your wealth grow. You can afford to take more risks than someone who's approaching retirement or is already there.

All your retirement-plan money is going to be in Bucket Nos. 2 or 3. If you're, say, 30 years old and have a secure, well-paying job, you theoretically could put all your retirement assets in your Bucket No. 3—in other words, you *could* load up on stocks and real estate and let them appreciate.

But I don't recommend that even for a carefree 30-year-old. A better plan would be to put 20% of your retirement assets in, say, tax-free muni bonds in Bucket No. 2 and the remaining 80% in the Bucket No. 3 stocks and real estate. Then you wouldn't lose all that much return in exchange for much less volatility. Also, if the stock market were to go into steep decline, you might want to tap into Bucket No. 2 to take advantage of the next bounce.

You couldn't do that if you didn't have at least some safe money on the sidelines.

If you are working now, you're probably putting money into a 401(k), an IRA, a Roth IRA, a SEP, or some other retirement plan. (If you aren't, you *should* be.) If retirement is still 10 or 15 years off, your asset-allocation model might feature an overweight Bucket No. 3, an underweight Bucket No. 2, and perhaps nothing in Bucket No. 1 because you don't need an income apart from your salary. The amount of time you leave your money in Bucket Nos. 2 and 3 could be longer or shorter than in our example, depending on when you want to retire.

But while you may not yet need income, you *will* need safety. So as you get closer and closer to retirement, you probably will want to swell your Bucket No. 2 to make sure you have a certain amount of "safe" money.

There's a real danger in not doing so. For instance, imagine somebody who retired in the year 2000 and had most of his or her retirement money in Bucket No. 3 and most of that tied up in tech stocks. (That wouldn't happen if you adhere to our asset-allocation model. But, hey, there are always mavericks who don't follow instructions!) Even the best such tech stocks—for instance, Intel, Cisco, and Sun Microsystems—took a terrific hit in 2000 and early 2001. Those are great companies, but it may take several years for a relatively new owner of those stocks to get his or her money back.

Thus, a tech-stock-heavy retirement portfolio would have been a disaster if the year 2000—or shortly thereafter—was when you were going to need the dough. In fact, I have fielded scores of telephone calls on my radio talk-show from individuals retired or nearing retirement who were overweighted in tech stocks and are now forced into either postponing retirement, going back to work, or acquiring a taste for dog food.

So, please, don't look for the quick buck, the fast turn-around. In fact, if you're going to buy stocks, even good ones, you'd better plan on owning them for, say, 10 to 15 years or more. Only that way will the market risk diminish to something manageable.

❑ **Nearing retirement.**

Planning gets a bit more critical as you approach retirement. One of the key questions: *What to do about Social Security?*

If you start drawing your Social Security check, your need for income from Bucket No. 1 and Bucket No. 2 will likely fall. So you might be able to divert some of your Bucket No. 1 funds to Buckets Nos. 2 or 3. You might also be able to lengthen the amount of time you leave money in Bucket No. 3. (Remember, the longer you leave it in, the more likely it'll grow and the less risk you face of losing money.)

When should you start drawing down your Social Security account? You can draw a partial benefit at age 62. That amounts to about 80% of the fuller benefit you'd receive if you wait until the normal retirement age of 65–67.

Does it make sense to get the benefit as soon as possible? Generally, yes. (The IRS used to penalize those who worked after age 65. But new rules generally allow working seniors to collect full Social Security benefits. New IRS rules also have lengthened life-expectancy schedules, thus reducing the post-age-70½ required minimum distribution for those with tax-deferred retirement plans. That means retirees can let more of their IRA nest-eggs grow tax-deferred for a longer time.)

As your retirement nears, you'll want to begin de-emphasizing Bucket No. 3. In short, you're going to want more income and less risk exposure to stocks.

❏ **Upon retirement.**

Once you retire, you probably will want to siphon money out of Bucket No. 3 and feed Bucket Nos. 1 and 2. But keep in mind that no matter if you're a retiree or a pre-retiree, your individual circumstance may dictate changes to our model.

For example, your estate plan might suggest how your money is invested. If you had, say, a $75,000 pension from your former employer, you might not need a Bucket No. 1 at all. Or maybe not even a Bucket No. 2. You might just live off the pension and put all Buckets money into a Bucket No. 3 that would be strictly for your kids' or your grandkids' inheritance.

Or, how you invested that Bucket No. 3 might be influenced by taxability. For instance, if that bucket is personal money (as opposed to a retirement plan), you might want all stocks there. That way you get a more favorable long-term capital-gains tax treatment if you want to get your hands on the money before you die. And then after you're gone, the kids inherit the gains free of income tax.

On the other hand, if Bucket No. 3 is an IRA, you might want it to contain the type of stocks that spin off taxable income like REITs, growth-and-income funds, and high-turnover mutual funds. That way you don't need to worry about taxation because an IRA is already tax-sheltered until the money is withdrawn. Any other Bucket No. 3 money outside your IRA and in your personal account could contain individual stocks, tax-managed mutual funds, or index funds because these are usually low-turnover funds and fairly tax efficient.

Thus, you hold the types of assets more likely to produce an ordinary-income tax hit in your IRA and those with the potential to receive long-term capital-gains tax treatment in your personal account. With ordinary-income rates in the high 30%-range (plus possible state income taxes) and capital-gains rates as low as 8% and as high as 20%, divvying up your Buckets in a tax-efficient manner is very important.

The joys of tax management

As you can see, everybody's situation is going to be different. For one person an annuity may be a great idea and for another it may be terrible. Ditto with muni bonds, real estate, or any other kind of investment. All of which leads us to some advanced bucketeering, the motto of which might be . . .

Lucia's Law | 25

The easiest way to make money is to stop losing it.

Many times, with proper planning, you can stay in a lower tax bracket. For example, let's say you and your spouse have a $1-million portfolio spread among CDs ($300,000), government bonds ($300,000), and retail mutual funds ($400,000) that are not tax-efficient. In other words, you are getting creamed each year with Form 1099s for short-term capital gains and dividends. Further, let's say the CDs earn 6% (about $18,000 a year), the bonds 7% ($21,000), and the funds produce income of about $20,000 from dividends and short-term capital gains.

That's ordinary income from your investments of $59,000. Add to that, say, a $30,000 pension, and you're looking at a taxable income of $89,000—which would put you firmly in the 28% federal marginal tax bracket. (I live in California, so if this were me, I'd have to add a 9.3% marginal state tax bracket, too.)

But with just a few changes, you could get a radically different result. For example, you could switch from government bonds to tax-free bonds. That would reduce taxes on your bonds to nothing. Further, you could put the CDs into a tax-deferred annuity, or if you need income, into an immediate annuity, which would reduce taxable income there to around $5,000. And you could tax-manage the mutual funds and maybe get that taxable income down to about $8,000 or less. Now your investment income is $13,000. Add that to your pension, and you get a gross taxable income of $43,000. *Voila!* Now you're in the 15% marginal tax bracket.

Instead of paying 28% in taxes on a portion of your income, you now owe 15% on that portion. That's a big difference. Or, to put it another way, you're earning an additional 13% and all you did was tax-manage your accounts. The point is: You can legally manipulate your tax situation considerably by just using various tax-favored investment vehicles and some fairly sophisticated tax-management techniques. A good financial advisor can help greatly in this area.

How you structure your ordinary income vs. long-term capital gains can be crucial. If, say, 50% of your portfolio is taxed now as ordinary income, that means the other 50% will be taxed at the long-term capital-gains rate. If you can tax-manage your portfolio so as to decrease to 10% or 20% the portion that's taxed as ordinary income, then 80% or 90% will be taxed at the lower, long-term capital-gains rate. That's a pretty good return, and you haven't added any money, just divvied it up differently.

In fact, in some cases you could go from a 39.6% tax rate to as low as 8% if you convert a taxable, ordinary-income asset to a long-term capital-gain asset and gift that asset to your grandkids. They can cash it in at their

10% or 15% tax bracket (if they're over age 14 . . . otherwise, the "kiddie tax" may kick in.) That's a tax-rate reduction of more than 31%—a pretty *big* number!

But unless you're an investment expert, you're probably not going to know enough about the ins and outs of tax planning and tax-managing your investments to make these kinds of changes for yourself. That's why it's critical that you have an advisor or an advisory team to go through all this stuff with you.

A powerful incentive

The lure of paying less tax can be a powerful incentive when you set up your buckets. Chart 8-1 shows how much more quickly a tax-deferred account grows over time.

As a result, sometimes you may wish to split your buckets between qualified (tax-deferred retirement accounts like an IRA) and non-qualified (taxable, personal money) retirement accounts, or have sub-buckets divided into retirement money and non-retirement money. With our progressive tax system, it's sometimes wise to pull money out of a qualified retirement plan because you're already in a low-tax bracket even if you aren't old enough to avoid the pre-age-59½ penalty tax (10%).

Take a case like this: A guy, age 54, has been making a $100,000-a-year salary but wants to semi-retire. He figures he needs something close to $70,000 a year to live, starting now for the rest of his life. He's got $400,000 in

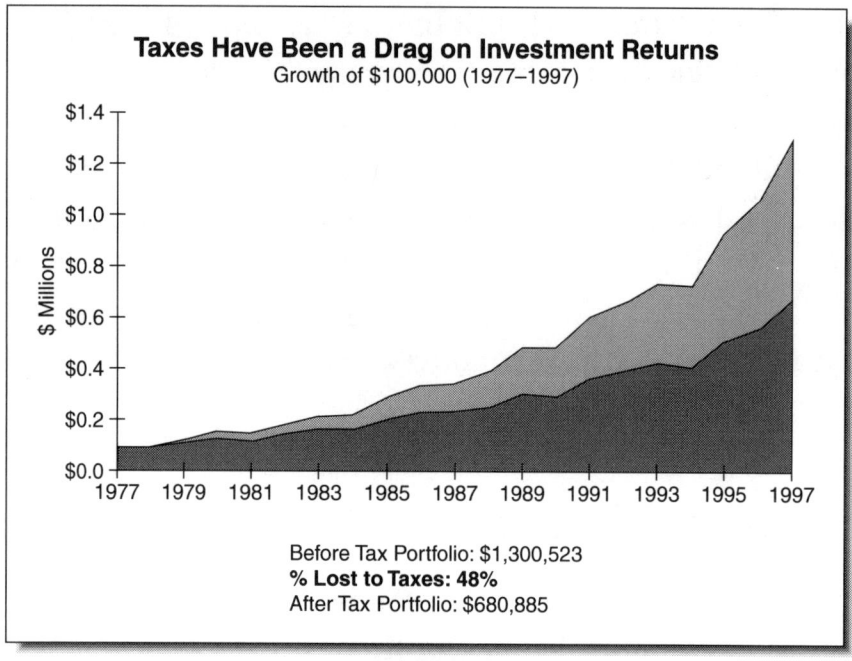

Chart 8-1

his IRA invested for growth (earning about 10%) and $200,000 in personal assets in CDs at 5%. His Social Security won't kick in for at least eight years.

Further, let's say he's started a part-time job which will pay $3,000 a month, or $36,000 annually. He has $30,000 in mortgage interest each year as well as other tax deductions (such as property tax, dependents, and the like) totaling $20,000. Thus, he's got $50,000 in write-offs.

Needing $70,000 a year to live on, he's got to come up with $34,000 more on top of his part-time salary. Where should that money come from? Most would say take it from the personal money and let the IRA grow. But I question that.

If he takes the $34,000 from his personal account, he is essentially in a negative tax bracket. His situation would look like this:

Salary	$36,000
Interest on CDs	10,000
	$46,000 total income
minus writeoffs	−50,000
= Taxable income	(4,000)
	0 taxes owed

This is foolish and not very tax efficient. Though he's not paying any income tax, he's also not very close to his income goal of $70,000, either. He can't carry forward to succeeding years those unused personal exemptions and deductions. But what he could do, though, is switch the $200,000 in taxable CDs into tax-managed growth accounts—and then leave them alone for the foreseeable future.

Then he can withdraw the needed $34,000 per year from his IRA account, which could be invested in a moderately safe portfolio. By doing so he creates enough ordinary income to use up the deductions in his low tax bracket.

(Now you're probably wondering: How can he tap into his IRA without a penalty if he's not yet 59½? He does so by taking out substantially equal payments over his life expectancy under what's known as a 72(t) election. More about this in the next chapter.)

Under this new plan, his situation would look like so:

Salary	$36,000	
Interest/Dividends (from tax-managed portfolio)	3,000	
IRA distribution	34,000	
	$73,000	total income
Minus writeoffs	−50,000	
= Taxable income	23,000	
	$ 3,450	taxes owed (approximate)

Do you see how he's been helped? Sure, he now pays about $3,450 in taxes (even less under the new tax bill passed in 2001), but he's moved a lot closer to his income goal. And his mix of assets hasn't changed. He still has $400,000 invested in the stock market earning 10% and $200,000 in CDs at 5%. The only thing that's changed is the way the personal and IRA money is allocated.

There are two further advantages:

• Much of the income from the $400,000 that now comes from the personal account will be taxed as capital gains, not ordinary income. Under current law, that means a maximum tax of 20% if you're in the 28% or higher tax bracket. (After the year 2001, the capital gains could drop to 18% if you hold the investment for more than five years. And in the 15% tax bracket, capital gains will drop from 10% to 8% for an investment held five years or more.)

- If he should die and his assets were held properly in trust, there may be a complete step up in the tax basis in his personal account. His spouse or heirs would never pay income tax on the gain from the $200,000 to whatever it grows to by the time he dies.

On the other hand, if he doesn't elect a 72(t) distribution and lives off his personal money, by the time he qualifies for Social Security, all of his non-salary/investment income will come from his IRA account. That's because he already will have spent all his personal income. Furthermore, his deductions will be lower, part of his Social Security will be subject to taxation, and when he reaches 70½, his RMD (required minimum distribution) will be higher.

If he continues to live a long time and didn't do the 72(t), he will face substantially more in income taxes at full retirement, especially if his house is eventually paid for and he loses that income-tax deduction. Also upon full retirement, when he presumably quits the part-time job, he will need to withdraw the full, inflation-indexed $70,000 less his Social Security.

All of this will then need to come out of his IRA, possibly sending him into a higher tax bracket. Whereas if he takes the needed money now out of the IRA and invests the rest he will be able to dramatically lower his taxes later.

So . . . the point of the exercise is to match the type of investment owned with the type of tax that's going to be paid.

A "legacy" sub-bucket

Here's another twist to the Bucket No. 3 setup, one I call the "legacy" sub-bucket. It's an especially good way to pass along the largest amount of inheritance with the smallest amount of tax. (This is different from the Legacy Asset mentioned in Chapter 4. That was a "cup" of money, equal to several months' expenses, that you keep outside of the buckets for an emergency.)

A lot of folks fail to take into account the effect of inflation on their estates. For instance, you might have $500,000 you're planning to leave your kids. And you diligently protect and preserve that sum for many years. The trouble is, those years of inflation take a toll. And when you die—say, 20 years later—that half mil isn't what it used to be. In purchasing power, you will have left your kin barely 50% of what you intended.

So what you can do is take some earnings from Bucket No. 3, such as the dividends paid out from the stock portfolio or REITs, and use this money to purchase a "second-to-die" life insurance policy. It insures both lives but pays off only at the second death. Thus, when the remaining spouse dies, the insurance proceeds can be used to (a) pay the estate taxes, if any; (b) replenish the Bucket No. 3 assets you've depleted over time; and/or (3) give your progeny an inflation hedge on the assets they inherit.

If you want a policy that is likely to mirror the performance of equities in Bucket No. 3, you could purchase a second-to-die *variable* life policy. It usually has a guaranteed death benefit (as long as you meet a minimum premium requirement) but the cash value depends on the performance of the underlying sub account, such as mutual funds. That way you're not giving up a whole lot from an investment-return standpoint. The cash values can be invested in the same kind of model portfolio as your Bucket No. 3 would be invested in anyway.

So a legacy sub-bucket works best for folks who probably won't spend every last dime of earnings from their long-term portfolio and who want to leverage their nest-egg to keep pace with inflation and perhaps give their kids or grandkids a head start on their own financial security. It's an excellent way to go if you're in that situation, but it's complicated and you'll probably want to consult a team of advisors, including a tax attorney, CPA, CFP™, CLU, ChFC, or qualified life-insurance agent .

Another scenario

I am showing such examples not because they are a must for your Buckets, but rather because I want you to see why it's sometimes wise to use multiple buckets within buckets. That way, you can draw income from the most advantageous sub-bucket.

Here's another tax-planning scenario: If you were in a high-tax bracket (39.6%), you might put your Bucket

No. 2 money in tax-free municipal bonds. In a market like the one we had in the spring, 2001 when interest rates seemed to be headed down, a short- or intermediate-term muni probably would be better for Bucket No. 2 than a tax-deferred annuity.

But on the other hand, if you're drawing Social Security and trying to avoid paying taxes on those payments, tax-free munis don't work so well. That's because the income they produce is an add-back to your modified adjusted gross income (MAGI), but the income from tax-deferred annuities is not. So if you were trying to get your Social Security tax-free, an annuity will work better than munis.

Theoretically, you can even add bonds to your Bucket No. 3, though I usually don't recommend that. Why? Because we're investing for long-term growth. Unless you think bonds will add more to your return, diluting your Bucket No. 3 with bonds isn't a good idea. Some conservative investors may want to look at some long-bond strategies in this bucket. But in my opinion, they can be as volatile as stocks and may not give you the stability and growth you're seeking. Besides, to make real money in bonds you either must use leverage (borrowing) or timing, neither of which I recommend.

What does it all mean?

It means you probably can't do this stuff yourself. You need professional help if you're to get the best bang for your buck. The strategies are as varied as the situations. But here's one inviolate rule. Let's call it . . .

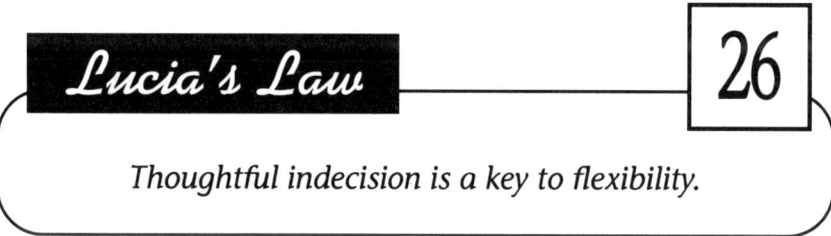

Lucia's Law   26

Thoughtful indecision is a key to flexibility.

In other words, stay nimble. Don't lock yourself into any one plan because your brother-in-law did, or because of something I wrote in this book, or because taking action—*any* action—seems better than contemplation.

Think—then go over all the options with your financial advisor(s).

Chapter 9

MANAGING YOUR BUCKETS IN GOOD TIMES AND BAD

L et's say you've got your *Buckets of Money*® all set up. So life is good and going according to plan. And then *something* happens!

It might be something *good*—like a rare stock-buying opportunity or inheriting some money. Or it might be something *bad*—such as prolonged poor health or a big tax liability. Or maybe it's neither good nor bad but just a contingency you must deal with—for example, you reach the age when you can, or must, draw down your IRA.

Any of those situations will probably prompt you to re-examine your Buckets plan. And in this chapter we'll look at what to do if those special circumstances arise.

Let's take the good news first.

A stock-buying opportunity. If the stock market plummeted 40%—not a theoretical possibility but a fact in 2000–2001!—and you've got a good chunk of "safe" money in your Bucket No. 2, what could or should you do? You obviously could do nothing, and that would be just fine. That's why we have safe money in Buckets Nos. 1 and 2, to get us through the rough spots. But usually the six months or a year or so after a market crash are very, very good recovery periods.

For individuals who can tolerate a bit more risk and want to possibly spice up their overall return, "reverse bucketing" may be a way to go. Thus, you could "borrow" some of your safe money in Bucket No. 2 and temporarily put it into Bucket No. 3, which is usually invested in a stock portfolio or mutual funds.

If the stock gods are in your favor and if the market bounces back in a year or two as it often—but *not always*— does, you may be able to significantly enhance your wealth. Then you could pull that money out of the equities in Bucket No. 3 and replenish your Bucket No. 2. It's like buying low and selling high.

Of course, you'd have to pay capital gains tax on those profits. But even so, depending on how much you invested and how well those stocks did, you might earn enough in a couple of years to give you perhaps four or five more years' worth of safe money in your Bucket No. 2.

This is high-risk, potentially high-reward strategy that's not for everyone—and certainly shouldn't be done often or without a great deal of thought. But potentially—if you and your advisor(s) decide to try it and all goes well—you could reinvigorate your Buckets and give yourself added years of safe, reliable income. In essence, you'd be taking a half-step backward in your Bucket No. 2 scenario in order to take a great leap forward.

Again, let me be clear: I'm not in favor of trying to time the market. But in cases of severe market downturns, like the 1973–74 decline or the "tech wreck" of 2000–01, stocks became relatively cheap. An investment made anywhere near the bottom likely paid handsome returns.

Getting a windfall. Or let's say your aunt dies and, much to your surprise, leaves you $100,000. How could you use that to bolster your Buckets? Well, that would be a nice problem. And there could be several equally pleasant solutions.

You could plunk the whole $100K into your Bucket No. 3 and let it grow. If you could afford to do so, that'd be the best, most long-term solution. That would work best if your Bucket No. 1 is churning out the income you need and your safe investments in Bucket No. 2 are doing what they're supposed to do, which is kick out a predictable, compounded return. If that's the case, then you can afford to squirrel away your inheritance on stocks and/or real estate in the long-term third bucket.

But depending where you are in the Buckets cycle and how it's working, you could also put some of your inheritance into Bucket Nos.1 and/or 2. For example, if inflation and expenses have drained Bucket No. 1 faster than you expected, perhaps you can give that bucket a big boost with some of auntie's money. That would also buy added time to allow Bucket No. 2 and Bucket No. 3 to grow.

Or maybe your Bucket No. 1 is producing the income you need, but you're worried about how much you're going to have in Bucket No. 2 when the time comes to empty it into the first Bucket. So maybe you'll want to use part of the inheritance to pump up Bucket No. 2.

Whatever you decide to do with your new-found gain, remember that *Buckets of Money*® is a long-term philosophy. A central part of that means putting a big chunk of money in Bucket No. 3 and leaving it there for as long you can. So, blessed with a windfall, think long-term, think Bucket No. 3 as much as possible.

Sad to say, not all our surprises are pleasant ones. You might also hit a big bump in the road. Let's take a look at how you might adjust your buckets if that should happen.

A prolonged illness. Maybe it's not even you who gets sick, but perhaps your parents or another family member. In any event, your earlier financial planning should help solve these problems. If that planning was done correctly, you should have talked to your advisor about such contingencies. You should have made it a point to provide for long-term health care for yourself and your family, taken into account your parents' situation, learned the Medicare rules and how Medicaid works in a long-term care situation.

But let's say you did all that—and *still* you're facing some big, unexpected costs, maybe hundreds of thousands of dollars worth. You must quickly figure out how to increase income: You must immediately change how your buckets are structured.

At that point you may have far more risk than you bargained for. Your Bucket No. 3 is loaded with stocks and maybe the market is rising nicely and your equities are doing well. But if your income needs to go up by, say, $3,000 a month to care for an ailing parent, you can't take the chance that the market won't flip-flop. You need to have a lot more safe money in case Wall Street quickly heads south. (We all know what happens when you have to pull money from a stock portfolio that's declining—you accelerate the loss. Just ask anybody who had to sell Intel stock in the year 2000 or 2001 just to live.)

So you're probably going to want to reapportion a good chunk of your Bucket No. 3 money into Buckets Nos. 1 and 2. How much? Enough to get you through this financial crisis. If that hypothetical $3,000 more a month will do it, then you can pretty easily figure how much more you're going to need in your Bucket No. 1. But don't forget: You're not just trying to meet your new obligation. You also want to lessen your exposure to risk by decreasing your Bucket No. 3; you can't continue to face that much risk when your need for current income is so acute.

Another path to consider is drawing down more of your IRA money. If you're over 59½, you could always opt to take a larger monthly distribution. (For most individuals, medical expenses that exceed 7½% of their adjusted gross income are deductible. So taking taxable funds out of your IRA could be offset in part by deductible medical costs, making the bulk of the IRA distribution "tax free.") The IRA distribution rules are there to make sure you withdraw the bare minimum; you can take out *more* than that. Even if you're not 59½, tapping your IRA and paying the 10% penalty or using a 72(t) election might be worth it if the consequences of not doing so are sufficiently severe.

Other alternatives might include taking out a home-equity loan, borrowing against your brokerage account, or in a severe case, even signing up for a reverse mortgage in which, in effect, you'd be drawing down the equity in your home to get you over this financial rough spot. (Reverse mortgages usually are not available if you're under age 65.)

But any way you slice it, this crisis is a sorry state of affairs. Bucket No. 3 should be growing, not shrinking. But sometimes you gotta do what you gotta do. With any kind of luck, perhaps the cash emergency will be short-lived, and you can restore your buckets to their proper proportion.

A big, one-time liability. Maybe it's not a medical emergency that slams you, but a financial one. Perhaps you're on the losing end of a lawsuit or are hit with a huge tax judgment or some other kind of setback that requires you to come up with cash, lots of cash.

Again, I would hope that financial planning would include the right kind of insurance for such a situation. But if it didn't and you need to raise the cash by dipping into your buckets, how would you do it?

Sad to say, you've probably got to dip again into that well we call Bucket No. 3. You need the assets in Bucket No. 1 to keep you in daily necessities. And that's backstopped by Bucket No. 2. So it's got to be No. 3 unless you are able to borrow some or all of the needed money, or the stock market has just gotten creamed and it makes more sense to risk giving up some of your safe money in Bucket No. 2 during the temporary setback. If, on the other hand, the market was on the rise and you expected it to continue its climb, you might consider borrowing at least part of the needed money if you had reason to believe your Bucket No. 3 stocks would grow at a faster clip than the interest rate on the loan.

But, as we know, this is a bit tricky. The stock market side of that equation can change in a heartbeat. And you could be left with a much smaller Bucket No. 3 as well as big loan payments. Be careful!

Drawing down your IRA

A more common dilemma is what to do with the Buckets when the time comes to start withdrawing your IRA money. As the law now reads, you *may* start that process when you reach 59½ years old. But you *must* do so when you become 70½.

Of course, being an IRS rule, it's much more complex than that. If you withdraw before age 59½, you'll likely get slapped with a 10% federal penalty in addition to federal and state taxes and maybe even a state penalty as well.

For all IRAs except the Roth, you must begin to withdraw the money by April 1 of the year following the year in which you turn 70½. (Failure to make the timely withdrawal will cost you—*are you ready for this?*—a 50% penalty.) The withdrawals—or "distributions" as they're known—are intended to last a lifetime. So you base your distributions on your (or your spouse's) life expectancy. IRS Publication 575—Pension and Annuity Income includes tables you can use to dope out your required distribution.

To use the simplest of examples, if the tables show you have 20 years to live and your IRA is $200,000, you would be required to take out (and be taxed as ordinary income by both the feds and the state) at least $10,000 this year. (1/20 = 5%; 5% × $200,000 = $10,000). The following year your minimum distributions increase (1/19, 1/18, 1/17, etc.) and if your account grows, you'll have to take out even more money.

The fallacy of common wisdom.

How you withdraw your IRA money and how you structure your Buckets for taxes will dramatically affect your retirement income. The common belief is: "Defer, defer, defer your taxes for as long as you can. Live off of your savings and don't tap into your IRAs until you absolutely have to at age 70½."

This mantra is accurate for some and foolish for others. Or as I sometimes say:

Lucia's Law 27

Absolute rules are created to allow us to escape thinking in exceptional situations.

Or, its corollary:

Lucia's Law 28

Fools rush in where fools have been before.

In short, deferring the withdrawal of IRA money accounts always makes sense—*except* if you can take money out in a low tax-bracket now instead of a higher bracket later. For example, let's say we have a married couple, age 62, with $50,000 in a money-market fund for emergencies as well as $200,000 in CDs. They have another $200,000 in stocks in an IRA. In addition, they receive $18,000 yearly in Social Security benefits and have a pension that pays them $18,000.

According to conventional wisdom, they should live off of the income from their $250,000 in bank accounts (the $50,000 in emergency money plus the $200,000 in CDs) and continue to invest their IRA in stocks until they are forced to take minimum IRA distributions at age 70½.

Their income and tax situation now looks something like this:

NOW

	Receive Yearly	Amount Taxable
Pension	18,000	18,000
Social Security Income	18,000	9,000
$50,000 Money Market (at 5%)	2,500	2,500
$200,000 CD (at 6%)	12,000	12,000
$200,000 IRA (stocks)	0	0
Total Income	$ 50,500	$ 41,500
Minus Write-offs/Personal Exemptions		− 16,500
Taxable Income		$ 25,000
Tax due		$ 3,750

On the surface this looks great. The IRA isn't paying out yet—it's compounding tax-free as IRAs are supposed to do. Meanwhile, the couple is in the 15% tax bracket and paying only $3,750 in taxes each year. Even if they Bucketize the $250,000 in personal assets, their tax situation will not change dramatically.

Assuming their stocks earn 12% over the next 8½ years (when the couple turns 70½), their IRA will be worth something on the order of $500,000. If we assume a life expectancy of 20 more years, they will need to make a minimum distribution of about $20,000 in the first year and increasing every year thereafter.

Thus, if they remain on the present course, their situation would look something like this in eight years:

AT AGE 70½ IF STAY ON PRESENT COURSE

	Receive Yearly	Amount Taxable
Pension	18,000	18,000
Social Security Income	18,000	15,300
$50,000 Money Market (at 5%)	2,500	2,500
$200,000 CD (at 6%)	12,000	12,000
$500,000 IRA (stocks) RMD (required minimum distribution)	19,100	19,100
Total Income	$ 69,600	$ 66,900
Minus Write-offs/Personal Exemptions		− 18,300
Taxable Income		$ 48,600
Tax due		$ 7,732

So, adding that $19,100 IRA distribution will cause their tax bill to more than double. They'll pay taxes of $7,732 vs. a tax of $3,750 that they were previously paying.

But let's take a look at how they might do better with a smart *Buckets of Money*® strategy. What they could do is:

- Put the $50,000 emergency fund in a tax-free money-market fund. That'll reduce the interest, of course, but also will contribute to reducing the tax bill.
- Convert the $200,000 in CDs to a well-diversified, tax-managed, all-stock portfolio with the objective

of long-term growth subject to long-term capital-gains tax when sold. They would call that their Bucket No. 3.

• Convert the IRA stock assets into safe investments funding Bucket Nos.1 and 2 (*e.g.,* bonds and CDs) and take the income from the IRA to meet their needs, at least to the extent of using up their 15% tax bracket. (It's good to use up that money now because otherwise the income will be received in the 28% bracket later.)

So under a scenario in which we tax-manage the portfolio but keep the income roughly the same, the couple's situation for the next eight years would look something like this:

NOW . . . IF TAX-MANAGED/BUCKETIZED

	Receive Yearly	Amount Taxable
Pension	**18,000**	**18,000**
Social Security Income	**18,000**	**9,000**
$50,000 tax-free money market (at 3%)	**1,500**	**0**
$200,000 Tax-Managed Stock Portfolio (Bucket No. 3) (figuring 1.5% dividend partially reinvested)	**3,000**	**3,000**
$200,000 IRA CDs/bonds (at 6%) (Bucket Nos. 1 and 2)	**12,000**	**12,000**
Total Income	**$ 52,500**	**$ 42,000**
Minus Write-offs/Personal Exemptions		**– 16,500**
Taxable Income		**$ 25,500**
Tax due		**$ 3,825**

So though the couple still has roughly the same amount to spend ($52,500 vs. $50,500), they have positioned themselves better for that time when they must draw down their IRA. They also effectively used the 15% tax bracket to their advantage in structuring their buckets.

So with this new, tax-managed structure, their situation at age 70½ (when they must start taking distributions from their IRA) will look thusly:

AT AGE 70½ IF TAX-MANAGED/BUCKETIZED

	Receive Yearly	Amount Taxable
Pension	18,000	18,000
Social Security Income	18,000	9,000
$50,000 tax-free money market (at 3%)	1,500	0
$470,000 Tax-Managed Stock Portfolio (Bucket No. 3) (figuring 1.5% annual dividend partially reinvested)	7,050	7,050
$200,000 IRA CDs/bonds (at 6%) (Bucket Nos. 1 and 2) RMD (required minimum distribution)	7,635	7,635
Total Income	$ 52,185	$ 41,685
Minus Write-offs/Personal Exemptions		– 18,300
Taxable Income		$ 23,385
Tax due		$ 3,508

Note that the IRA distribution can be reduced as the dividend on the stock portfolio increases. This is good because the couple meets their income needs without additional distributions—and thus, without additional taxes.

The bottom line? They'll pay less than half the tax ($3,508 vs. $7,732) per year when they turn 70½ than if they hadn't re-structured their income.

Yet another big advantage

There's another big advantage this hypothetical couple would get if they took income out of the IRA while investing personal assets for growth. That happens when the husband or wife dies.

If they had stuck with the original, non-tax-managed plan, the surviving spouse would have had to pay more than double the amount of income taxes. Assuming one spouse dies at 70½, that picture would have looked like this:

AT AGE 70½, SURVIVING SPOUSE, NON-TAX-MANAGED ACCOUNTS

	Receive Yearly	Amount Taxable
Pension	18,000	18,000
Social Security Income	12,000	10,200
$50,000 money market (at 5%)	2,500	2,500
$200,000 CDs/bonds (at 6%)	12,000	12,000
$500,000 IRA (stocks) RMD (required minimum distribution)	19,100	19,100
Total Income	$ 63,600	$ 61,800

Minus Write-offs/Personal Exemptions	− 14,700
Taxable income	**$ 47,100**
Tax due	**$ 9,671**

Compare that to the tax bite the surviving spouse faces if the couple had gone to a tax-managed/Buckets plan:

AT AGE 70½, SURVIVING SPOUSE, TAX-MANAGED ACCOUNTS

	Receive Yearly	Amount Taxable
Pension	18,000	18,000
Social Security Income	12,000	10,200
$50,000 tax-free money market (at 3%)	1,500	0
$470,000 Tax-Managed Stock Portfolio (Bucket No. 3) (figuring 1.5% annual dividend partially reinvested)	7,050	7,050
$200,000 IRA CDs/bonds (at 6%)(Bucket Nos. 1 and 2) RMD (required minimum distribution)	7,635	7,635
Total Income	**$ 46,185**	**$ 42,885**
Minus Write-offs/Personal Exemptions		− 14,700
Taxable Income		**$ 28,185**
Tax due		**$ 4,375**

In addition, the surviving spouse has access to the $470,000 in the stock portfolio free of capital-gains taxes. That's because assets held properly in a personal account receive a step-up in tax basis upon the death of a spouse; assets held in an IRA do not. Thus, if the pair had stuck with the non-tax-managed plan, the stock portfolio then in the IRA would have been taxed upon receipt by the survivor or the ultimate heirs. That tax could be as high as 39.6% federal, plus a potential state tax as well.

The point is, it's crucial to study the impact of taxes on each bucket. A further point, of course, is that it makes sense to have a professional advise you before setting up any Buckets plan.

Getting beyond the box

As the popular phrase goes, sometimes it pays to think "out of the box." For example, even if you're under 59½, there may be times when it may be advantageous to draw down your IRA.

Let's say you're 53 years old and have an IRA balance of $200,000 as well as another $200,000 in personal money. You need $1,000 a month, and you're in a low-tax bracket because of business-loss carry forward.

You might be able to employ IRS Code Section 72(t), under which you can annuitize the withdrawal of money from your IRA without having to pay a penalty. If you're 53, you have roughly a 30-year life expectancy. Figuring a 7.5% growth rate on your IRA, you could expect to withdraw about $16,800 a year or roughly $1,400 a month.

If you could take $1,400 a month out of your IRA penalty-free and that came out in the 15% tax bracket, you could let the $200,000 in personal money grow at long-term capital gains rates and have it be tax-free at death. That might turn out to be a plus.

Another example: You're a 50-year-old with $500,000 in an IRA and $350,000 in personal money. You want to retire or semi-retire, and you need $40,000 to $50,000 a year to live on.

Your life expectancy is 33 years. Figuring a 7.5% return, you could take $41,000 annually out of the IRA before you're 59½. That's taxable as ordinary income, but there are no penalties for these early withdrawals if you use the 72(t) election.

In this example, you invest your $350,000 in personal money for growth. By the time you're 59½, your personal money, which let's say has been growing at 10%, is now up to $630,000 (and will be taxed at the lesser capital-gains rate when withdrawn, or will be tax-free at death). Your IRA is still around $500,000 (because the 7.5% growth rate matched your 7.5% annual withdrawal.)

What have you accomplished? Well, in addition to having enjoyed the $40,000 per year to live on, you still have $500,000 in IRA money and $630,000 in the more tax-efficient personal account.

If you hadn't done the 72(t), you would have drawn down much of your personal account. Meanwhile, your IRA would have grown to about $1.3 million by the time you reach 70—which means you'd be forced to take a minimum distribution in a higher income-tax bracket.

Or if you're 49 years old and have all your money—$400,000, let's say—in IRAs. You have no personal investments. You want to diversify, so you're thinking of buying a condo or apartment building. You've got a 34-year life expectancy. Figuring 7.5% growth on your $400,000 IRA, you could, under Code Section 72(t), draw down your IRA by $32,500.

You could take this $32,500 and re-diversify into real estate. Why? Because if you buy real estate with your personal (not IRA) account, you would get long-term capital-gains tax treatment. Further, you would have leverage on the real estate as well as depreciation and other tax deductions. Thus, with a relatively small investment, you could control property worth much more and get added tax benefits. That, of course, accelerates the potential for return.

Or, if you wanted to buy a serious piece of real estate, you could even borrow, say, $500,000 and use the IRA draw-down to pay off the loan over time. If you've got real estate that grows at 5% annually, you would be earning $25,000 a year on a $35,000 investment. And in this example, the $32,500 withdrawn from the IRA would be offset by a mortgage deduction on the $500,000 loan, reducing the tax liability on your 72(t) distribution. Obviously, this is a risky strategy that's not for everybody. But it could produce a heckuva rate of return if you can find the right property.

Making dreams come true

I had a situation not long ago where a couple with three small children wanted to move to a larger home but were afraid the new mortgage would be too steep to handle. They had very little cash personally but had handsome IRA and 401(k) plans. We decided that living today was just as important as living well at retirement. So we spun off enough money into a separate IRA, did a 72(t) election, and produced a $1,500-per-month distribution.

They were used to paying $3,000 a month in mortgage costs. The new home was $4,500 per month. So it worked out perfectly because their 72(t) IRA gave them just what they needed. This distribution was taxable, but the extra interest they were going to pay on the new mortgage offset the taxable income from the IRA.

They're now living happily in their new, larger home. The kids play in the new yard, and the whole family swims in the new pool and enjoys barbecue on the new deck—all without financial stress because their out-of-pocket expense is identical to what it was in the old house. I was clearly their hero, which is why I *love* doing financial planning. Every so often you can watch dreams come true!

The classic case

The whole idea is to take money out of your portfolio with the least impact on taxes. That's why we use the buckets or even fractionalize the buckets based on how much income we'll actually need to live on and how much we think our overall assets are worth.

The classic case is a teacher or government worker. He or she typically has a defined-benefit pension, a 401(k), a

403(b), or similar kind of pre-tax retirement-savings plan, possibly a pre-tax deferred compensation package (457 plan) and personal IRAs. So, basically, every penny he takes out of those assets upon retirement is taxable.

This individual really needs to begin saving some post-tax money. Perhaps he or she could take advantage of Roth IRAs for tax-free growth if left alone until after age 59½. Even reducing the amount of discretionary dollars invested in pre-tax plans makes sense if you take an equal amount and invest it in a post-tax account. This way, one builds both pre- and post-tax assets so when it comes time to Bucketize, you can blend these two assets in order to reduce the tax bite.

The moral of these stories isn't that you should be intent on drawing down your IRA before age 59½ or that you should jump into real estate or jump into anything else. The point is that the possibilities are infinite, depending on your aspirations and the acumen of both you and your advisor. One of the major tasks you'll want to use your advisor for is finding a strategy that will work for you whether you're fully retired and need your investment income to live on, or are in the pre-retirement phase and want to enhance your income today or upon retirement.

Finding the right withdrawal strategy

Too few people know—or think much about—how to plan their investment withdrawals during retirement. *Buckets of Money*® is a sound, conservative strategy that helps you avoid the common mistake of having either too little exposure to stocks (thus, lacking protection against inflation) or too much (making you overly vulnerable to market whims.) But it's not a guaranteed money machine; it still needs to be managed prudently.

So when the time comes to draw down your IRA and/or Bucket No. 3, beware of averages. Averages—such as the stock market's long-term average annual gain of 10+%—are helpful, but they can be hugely deceiving. (Remember the old joke about the guy who had his head in the oven and his feet in the refrigerator? *On average,* he felt quite comfortable!) The future is never exactly like the past. In truth, there are few "average" years, and variables abound—including how long you will live, the market's rise and fall, and the pace of inflation.

So how much can you safely withdraw from your portfolio each year? Probably less than you think. Why? Because the average stock-market results are just that, an average. It's a mistake to just focus on the long-run average rates of return and not think about what can go wrong.

Further, even if a year did turn out to be "average," that doesn't mean *your* return will be. Not everybody will enjoy the same good returns. Some investors will get significantly below-average results. That's *why* it's an average!

When you look at returns over, say, 50 years, the ups and downs sort of balance out. But when you start pulling out money in retirement, those ups and downs really matter. Let's say you have a $500,000 stock portfolio. You know the stock market grows long-term an average of more than 10% a year. So you figure you can withdraw $50,000 a year and still keep a half million in your account.

But that first year the market dips 20% (a relatively modest decline by recent standards), and your total falls to $360,000 (deducting your $50,000 plus 20% of the remaining $450,000).

If the market and your account bounce back 20% the following year, the *average* market gain/loss for the past two years is 0. But your account is at only $382,000 after you take out another $50,000. Despite what the averages say is a break-even couple of years, you're down $118,000 that you may never get back. In fact, if the market has several such bad years while you're still taking out 10%, you could go broke in a surprisingly short time!

Further, the sequence of the returns also matters. Whether the up years come at the beginning, middle, or end of your retirement years makes a big difference. For example, retire just before a bull market, set up your Buckets, and you may live well and pass on a handsome sum to your heirs. Retire just before a bear market and with the same nest egg, same three Buckets, same spending rate, you could easily outlive your money. Again, that's because you're going to be drawing down on a shrinking amount.

In short, real life is more chaotic than your pocket calculator indicates. So you need to work carefully with your financial planner on various scenarios that anticipate a few shocks along the way.

Here are some suggestions to take into that meeting:

- Assume you'll live to 100.
- Run several projections, including some with very conservative returns so you get an idea of the range of outcomes you might face. Do the calculations year by year with actual returns rather than the average return for the period. (Ask your adviser to use something called "Monte Carlo simulation." This takes into account a number of random performance scenarios and gives you the probability of success or failure.)
- Expect a long-term return of no more than 8%–9% on your stock investments after you retire. (If that turns out to be low, you can attribute the jump in value to your brilliance as an investor!)
- Get your planner to show you how, by adjusting the mixture of stocks and bonds in your portfolio, you can affect the probability that your money will last as long as you do. Then choose a risk factor that's comfortable for you.
- But, if possible, plan to withdraw no more than 5%–6% per year of your diversified portfolio's growing value. This won't produce a fixed income but it should help prevent you from running out of money.

Work with your planner and respect his or her judgment. But make it clear you'd rather be safe than sorry.

Obviously, a key in all this is to hire a really sharp, talented advisor, someone who understands the architecture of your financial plan and the architecture of investments. That kind of knowledge and flexibility counts for a lot. In fact, in some cases it can even make up for investment under-performance.

How do you find such a person? I'm glad you asked that . . . because that's what we're going to look at next.

Chapter 10

FINDING THE RIGHT FINANCIAL PLANNER

If you're uncommonly cool and clear-headed, you're probably thinking after reading the last chapter: *Sure, I understand all that. Now let's get started with some serious wealth-building!*

O.K., so much for fantasy. If you're like most everyone I know, your thoughts are more along the lines of: *Arrgghhh! This is complicated stuff—all those situations, all those possible tax consequences, all those various strategies! How can I ever get a handle on this?*

How you can get a handle on it is by getting help. Most folks don't have the training, the time, or perhaps the temperament to do this kind of planning themselves. So if you want to do a good job with your portfolio, you're going to need to pick an able financial advisor or a team of advisors. Then you can sleep well knowing you've got a plan tailored for you and a portfolio that's fully diversified and minimally volatile.

Remember: Broad diversification and a multi-asset/ multi-style/multi-manager approach to investing is what will make your Bucket No. 3 work. And as a practical matter, you'll probably need an investment professional to help you attain that. In this chapter, we're going to look at ways to find such a person or persons.

For starters, let's review what we have said such an advisor would do. In general, he or she is someone who can help you take a step back and see the bigger picture, someone who can study your situation and devise a program that'll meet your goals. Specifically, the planner will:

- **Work with you to develop a plan.** This means, first, understanding your goals. Then, the advisor puts your plan and the recommendations in writing so there's absolutely nothing left for interpretation now or later. Next, the advisor selects the right kind of investments, insurance, estate planning, tax planning, trusts, budgeting, and other methods to reach those goals and fulfill the plan's recommendations.
- **Pick—or work with a money-manager selection firm to pick—good fund managers.** It's these money managers who will do the hands-on choosing of your specific investments.
- **Hold those managers to their style discipline.** That might be growth, value, large-cap, small-cap . . . whatever, but not overlapping.

- **Know how to judge a manager's performance.**
  Be familiar with the appropriate benchmarks and
  compare the managers' results to them.
- **Terminate those managers who consistently
  under-perform relative to their benchmarks.**
  This isn't fun but is sometimes necessary.
- **Keep up to date with changes in the financial world.** That might mean changes in interest
  rates, changes in kinds of investment vehicles, per-
  sonnel changes in the money-manager ranks . . .
  all sorts of changes.
- **Re-balance your investments.** The planner assists
  you in sticking to your asset-allocation model.
- **Tax-manage your portfolio.** The planner helps you
  keep your taxes as low as possible vis-a-vis your other
  objectives.

Not surprisingly, you're going to need to spend some
bucks to get this kind of help. But if you hire a really sharp
advisor, his or her performance should pay for itself—and
a lot more.

So . . . how do you find such a wizard? Well, first make
sure you know what you're looking for. If you don't want
a full-blown financial plan, if you just want someone to
give you investment advice, then almost any planner or
broker can do that. And in some states, almost anyone
can advertise himself as being a financial planner. So you
won't have any trouble finding one if you're aiming for
just, say, a stock- or mutual-fund picker.

But if—as I would strongly urge—you want a full-blown financial review and a real plan, you probably want to look for a CFP™, a ChFC, a CLU, a PFS, or some similar designation. Or at the very least, look for someone working hand in hand with a skilled, credentialed advisor.

What do all those letters mean?

What the abbreviations stand for is not as important as what they signify in a broader sense—that this person took the time and made the effort to study the field, subscribe to its code of ethics, and take continuing education courses.

But more important than the exact initials after his or her name is what kind of rapport you have with the planner . . . how knowledgeable he or she is . . . how interested he is in your situation . . . and how well you like and understand the plan he comes up with. Still, knowing a little about this alphabet soup may help you make a better choice.

First, some background: In the good ol' days, it was relatively easy to know whom to go to for help. A banker loaned cash, an insurance agent sold insurance, and a stockbroker peddled stocks and bonds. But several things have happened to change that. One, a lot of new products got introduced—everything from annuities to junk bonds, from foreign currency options to pork belly futures. Secondly, new types of salespeople sprouted up to sell both the old and new investment vehicles. Further, the distinctions among those salespeople blurred, so that bankers now also sell stocks and stockbrokers now loan money and insurance agents now can get you into all manner of investments.

Thus, the task becomes not only *what* to buy but *from whom* to buy it. That's one of the big reasons for the popularity of financial planners. At their best, they help you cut through the clutter and make the best financial choices. But just because he or she is a financial planner—even a credentialed financial planner—doesn't guarantee a successful relationship.

The keys to finding the right financial planner include locating someone (1) whom you are comfortable with (2) who is willing to explain your options and (3) who charges a reasonable fee/commission.

But, of course, that's not as simple as it sounds because financial planners come in a lot of different flavors. For starters, there are those alphabetical designations. And then there's the question of how planners are paid. Let's take those issues one by one:

Alphabetical designations. Some of the initials you see after a planner's name are there because of federal licensing requirements while others represent ways the industry seeks to market its services.

For example, planners who sell securities must hold a federal securities license. Most also are members of the National Association of Security Dealers (NASD), a quasi-governmental agency that regulates the industry.

Any person who provides financial planning also must be a Registered Investment Advisor. That means he is registered with a different federal agency, the Securities and Exchange Commission. He did so by filing a form, paying a fee, and showing that he understands SEC rules. While you should never work with anyone who's not registered (because it's a federal crime to be an unregistered planner), neither should you take the designation oh-*so*-seriously because what it really means is that the registrant knows SEC procedures, not necessarily the finer points of financial planning.

The other designations are issued by the various financial industry associations, not by the government. Applicants must complete course work and meet other prerequisites to be awarded these designations, which include:

CFP™—This well-known set of initials stands for Certified Financial Planner and is earned by those who take a two-year course, pass a rigorous two-day examination, and meet continuing-education requirements.

ChFC—Chartered Financial Consultant is a designation given usually to insurance agents or financial planners who undergo a two-year program and complete exams and continuing education. Many ChFCs are also CLUs, or Chartered Life Underwriters, which involves a similar course of study and continuing education.

CFS—A Certified Fund Specialist has taken a course and exam centering on the selection and monitoring of mutual funds.

CMFC—Like CFS, this designation reflects the advisor's expertise in the mutual fund industry, but this one stands for Chartered Mutual Fund Counselor.

CRPC—A Chartered Retirement Planning Counselor specializes in retirement planning issues.

RFC—Registered Financial Consultants must meet education and licensing requirements and take a minimum of 40 hours of professional education each year. That's roughly two to four times as much as the other designations require.

PFS—This designation as a Personal Financial Specialist is offered to Certified Public Accountants (CPAs) who pass a test or hold the CFP™ or ChFC designation.

If your planner doesn't have any of those designations, then he or she at least ought to be working in tandem with somebody who does.

How they are paid. A great deal is written in the financial press about how financial planners are paid: commission-only, fee-only, or some combination. I'm not so sure it matters all that much. But just so you'll be fully informed, let me explain the pros and cons of each.

First, understand the difference between a financial planner and, say, a captive stockbroker or insurance agent.

The broker and agent usually will talk to you about their products and will give you lots of advice about which of their products might be best.

Planners, on the other hand, usually don't have proprietary products per se. What they do is take a comprehensive look at your situation, offer advice to help meet your goals, and then fill your needs with various non-proprietary products. But, as you'll see, some planners work for banks, brokerages, or insurance firms, or work as independent advisors. And they probably sell the same types of products as insurance agents or stock brokers.

Product sales aren't necessarily bad. After all, someone has to get you to act. But it's important for you to understand the compensation arrangement.

Commission-only planners. These planners almost always work for a bank, brokerage, or insurance company. But like planners elsewhere, they will ask about your income and expenses, your goals, your comfort level with risk, and so on, before suggesting "appropriate" investments. They would argue that instead of paying two fees—one to hire a planner and one to a broker to buy the investments—you can do one-stop shopping. You can just hire the commission-only planner and only pay when he makes a transaction for you. Others contend the commission-only planner is naturally biased toward his firm's products and thus has a built-in conflict of interest.

I know and trust many commission-only planners. If you can find the right one, you may save some money in the long run. However, I also know a few whom I wouldn't trust with the equity in my old pair of wingtips.

Pure fee-only planners. These planners get a fee to make the same kind of analysis and to give you recommendations. Much like an attorney, they charge for their service and their time. But because they have nothing to sell, you go to someone else to actually purchase the investment. The planner's fee may be an hourly rate (say, $100 or more per hour) or a flat fee (perhaps several thousand dollars.) They neither receive a commission nor place assets under management for a fee.

Advocates of pure fee-only planning say it's free of conflict of interest. But critics argue that you still need to pay a commission or sales charge to a broker to implement the plan. The fact that you're paying twice, they say, doesn't necessarily make the advice any better or the process cheaper or more pleasurable.

But, in any event, these types of advisors or advisory firms are rare.

Fee-only planner. These planners make the same kind of analysis and give you recommendations, but they usually also charge an asset-based fee on the assets they place under management. Most belong to a professional organization and are held to very strict standards. However, "fee only" is sometimes disguised as a rolling, annual commission and may, in fact, turn out to be more expensive than if you paid a load in the first place.

Combination fee/commission. This is a common arrangement in which planners charge you for the analysis, then sell you the investments and either receive a commission or a fee based on the assets under management or on how well your portfolio performs. These commission-like "asset-management fees" are preferred by some consumers because they avoid up-front commissions. Planners also like asset-management fees because they provide a steady stream of income, whether the investor is trading or not. Where asset-management fees become a problem is when the percentage is too high (say, above 2%) and when yet other fees are tacked on.

Fee-offset. These are advisors who charge a fee, and if you choose to do business with them, "rebate," or offset, the fee against their commission. This avoids double-dipping, but in some respect cheapens the plan itself and may skew it toward the products the advisor wants to sell.

Me? I don't think the whole debate amounts to much. In fact, I believe it's ludicrous to say that a fee-only advisor is necessarily better than someone who charges a commission. So many aspects of financial planning—such as integrity and knowledge—are so much more important. The truth is, you're going to pay either way, and in some cases you may end up paying more to a fee-only advisor.

So the bottom line is this: If you hire the right advisor, it shouldn't matter how he or she is paid. If he does a good job, he'll be worth the fee and/or commission. If he doesn't do a good job, then whatever way you paid him will be misspent. You don't want to overpay (keep that 2% figure in mind), but as to the form of payment, who cares?

What I believe is more important is that the planner discloses fully his financial arrangement. I'd almost like to see a new "FD" designation, along the lines of CFP™-FD or CFC-FD. The FD would stand for "Full Disclosure," which means the planner shows prospective clients how he is paid, how often he is paid, how much he is paid and by whom. That might be the most helpful designation of them all.

In any case, you should insist on full disclosure when working with any financial advisor.

Where to find a planner

Just as you would before hiring a plumber or a brain surgeon, make an effort to ask around. Query friends or co-workers whose judgment you respect and whose financial situation and risk-sensitivity is somewhat akin to yours.

Many advisors give free seminars. This can be a way to not only learn more about investing but also check out the planners themselves. These seminars often are advertised in the newspaper or on radio-TV or through flyers that come in the mail.

You could always use the Yellow Pages, of course, and the Internet now provides another way to connect with the right planner. Web sites for the big financial-planning organizations, such as the National Association of Personal Financial Advisors (www.napfa.org) and the Financial Planning Association (www.fpanet.org), have search mechanisms to help connect you to their members who practice near where you live. In addition, MSN's Money-Central (http://moneycentral.msn.com) also has a device for helping you find planners by geographic preference. (As I write this book, I am personally credentialing financial advisors to help out my radio listeners around the country. That web site is www.24-7financial.com, which incidentally is a "pure fee-only" planning company.)

What to expect

Good planners will draw out needed information from you by asking questions. Their aim will be to figure out your objectives. They may also request copies of wills, trusts, partnership or pre-nuptial agreements, insurance, employee benefit manuals, investment information, and perhaps even ask you to draw up a budget and balance sheet listing everything you own and everything you owe.

But *you* ought to be asking questions, too. I recommend you interview at least three planners and ask them these 12 questions.

1. How long have they been in the business and how long have they been in your community? Planners who have roots in the community may be more cautious than johnny-come-latelys. Even more important is how long they've been planners.

You want someone who's been around long enough to have suffered through a bear market. Prior to the bear market of 2000–2001, a lot of younger planners hadn't experienced such a downturn. As a result, you could run into, say, a talented, aggressive 27-year-old planner who forgot about safe money, forgot about value, threw caution to the wind, and really overexposed his clients to risk. Many folks right now are paying the price for that and may need to delay retirement because their planner, having never experienced that sinking feeling of losing a lot of his clients' money, was too aggressive.

So you want to make sure your advisor has enough experience to deal with your situation. You want him or her to understand how you need safety as well as growth.

2. What will they do for you? Design a plan? Implement it? Both?

3. What is their investment philosophy? This is important. You don't want to be force-fed financial choices. Be clear what your goals are and how you'll be most comfortable getting there. You want to be sure your planner understands modern portfolio theory—that is, asset allocation—and isn't just trying to time the market, use gimmicks, try out risky strategies, or bet your money on his ability to pick "winner" stocks.

4. What kind of investments do they specialize in? Be wary if they talk just about insurance . . . or limited partnerships . . . or mutual funds . . . or any one investment vehicle to the exclusion of most others. In short, you want someone who is planning-driven, not product-driven. Then if the plan calls for one or more of the aforementioned products, you can respond accordingly.

5. Who is their typical client? Once you know that, then you can judge: Are you a good match with how much their average investor has to invest? Are you comfortable with roughly the same amount of risk? You also might ask to talk with some clients whose situations are similar to yours, especially those who have been through down years as well as up years with this planner.

What you'll want to find out from those clients is not so much the state of their investments but the state of their relationship with the planner. Has he or she kept them informed? Has he done what he promised? Has he exceeded expectations in some ways? How? Disappointed in others? How?

6. How will this relationship work? Who will make the decisions—you or the planners? What kind of paperwork will they send you? Do they require you to sign a contract? If so, how can you opt out if the relationship sours? How often will you meet face-to-face?

7. How are they paid? If by fee, what do the fees include? If by commission, how much will that likely be? Ask for a full, clear explanation because some planners claiming to be "fee only" actually receive commissions as well.

8. Have complaints been filed against them? Ask them directly. But also, especially if you have any doubts, check the National Association of Security Dealers (if they have a securities license), the state insurance commission (if they have an insurance license), and the SEC (to see if they are Registered Investment Advisors.)

All planners are supposed to give you a copy of Form ADV Part II, which is a statement they file with the SEC about their background, methods, and fees. But you may have to ask for it. You can also ask to see Part I, which they are not required to show you.

Part I discloses any history of criminality or regulatory sanctions as well as unsatisfied judgments, liens, and bankruptcies. Part I also tells the number of clients advised in the past year and total assets under management.

The SEC is in the process of making Form ADV Parts I and II available more easily and quickly on the Web (www.sec.gov). Investment advisors will be required to file an electronic version of Form ADV. (A disciplinary history of brokers at firms who are members of the NASD already is available online at www.nasd.com. But unlike Form ADV, the NASD records don't provide information about fees, business practices, educational background or potential conflicts of interest.)

9. Will the planner draw up a letter explaining exactly what's going to happen, including planning services and fees?

This should be part of the full disclosure I mentioned earlier.

10. Will they show you a sample financial plan? Seeing this may help you decide if they are preparing thorough plans or just crunching numbers into a software program, a task you could probably do yourself for much less money.

11. What kind of assumptions are they going to use in your plan? For example, will they use life expectancy as defined in some computer program—say, 78 years old—or will they use a more conservative approach and take you out to 100 years old or beyond? If they stipulate 78 and you live to age 100, those last 22 years could be rough!

And what kind of market-return assumptions? If they project more than 10% annual return for stocks (net, after their fees), that's too aggressive. Similarly, what kind of withdrawal scenario do they foresee? I've seen cases where planners had clients taking, for instance, 8% a year out of 100% equity portfolios. That's nuts! One or two down years and that portfolio is going to shrink faster than an ice cream cone in Phoenix in July.

12. Are they backed by a firm of size and stature? Is the planner part of an organization of some heft and reputation? Or is it a rinky-dink outfit that, should there be trouble, won't be of much help? With any kind of luck, this is an issue you'll never need to put to the test. But it wouldn't hurt to find the answer to this question: If the planner did run away to Tahiti with your money, would you get reimbursed by his or her organization?

Other things to check out

By using your eyes and ears when you visit a prospective planner, you can also connect some other dots. For example:

- *How big is the office and how's it run?* If the staff is too big, that'll drive up costs. If it's too small, you could have trouble getting your calls returned. Does the office appear to be neat and organized? Neither too luxurious nor too spartan?
- *Do they explain things well?* Can they make it simple enough for you to understand? Or are they hiding beneath too many technical terms and a blizzard of statistics?
- *Do they talk about you first?* They should find out about you before moving on to products that they believe would be good for you. A product-first approach suggests a planner who's perhaps more interested in peddling something than in coming up with a plan that matches your goals.

Getting started with a planner

Once you've found the financial planner for you, take good advantage of that opportunity. Be proactive, not passive. Seek to be a full partner in the discussions.

For starters, figure out how much income you're going to need from your Bucket No. 1. Don't necessarily take at face value those articles in the money magazines that say you'll need 75%—or 60% . . . or 80%—of your present-day income to live on when you retire. Instead, carefully review with the planner your current monthly cash flow. Factor in any costs you expect to incur down the road—more travel, perhaps, or different hobbies, or maybe a boat or a new car.

Then subtract any contributions you're now making to your retirement accounts and Social Security because you'll no longer be paying those once you retire. Also eliminate expenses normally associated with work—business clothes, lunches out, and commuting costs.

Subtract your mortgage payment, too, if your house will be paid for by then. But be sure to include inflation-adjusted homeowners' insurance and property taxes because those don't go away just because you pay off the mortgage.

Take into account you and your spouse's Social Security benefits and when you expect to receive them. And, of course, any other benefits—like a company pension, an annuity, or an inheritance—that might kick in later.

Once you've figured out just what you're going to need in Bucket No. 1, it's just a matter of arithmetic to tally how much you'll need in Bucket No. 2. And the rest—by far the largest portion of your assets, I hope—goes into the third bucket.

Then comes the "fun" part—doping out what kinds of investments will meet your Buckets objectives. Be patient. Be persistent. It'll take a little time and effort to do this right, but it's time and energy well spent. In fact, much better spent than just fretting about the future but not doing anything about it.

Or, as I sometimes say . . .

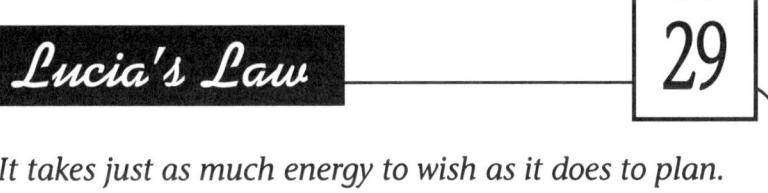

Lucia's Law | **29**

It takes just as much energy to wish as it does to plan.

And its corollary:

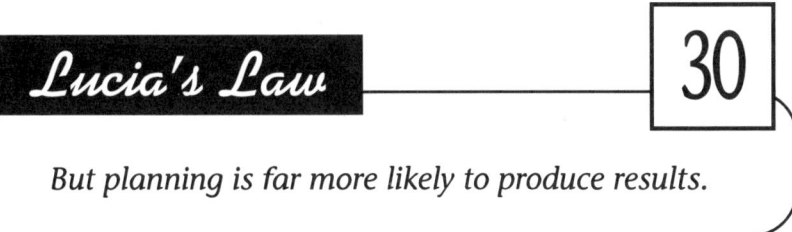

Lucia's Law | **30**

But planning is far more likely to produce results.

Planner vs. money manager

How do they differ? In short, a financial planner is a big-picture person who helps you with your strategy and who, among other things, can put you in touch with a money manager. A money manager actively oversees your investments on a day-to-day basis.

Sometimes a planner is also a money manager. But if I were you, I'd steer clear of those. Either job is a demanding one, and the odds are not good that someone can simultaneously do both well. Further, money managers tend to become experts in their own investing style—say, small caps, growth, or value stocks—and by definition, you as a diversified investor will want your portfolio to span multiple styles, not be concentrated on one. The way to get that diversification is to have a financial planner who will help you draw up a plan, set up your asset-allocation model, re-balance your portfolio, help you manage risk, and make sure you have enough liquidity. Then that planner can hire style-specific managers to invest your money in accord with your plan. Those money managers choose and buy the actual stocks.

How does the planner find these money managers? He or she may hire them directly or may work through a money-manager selection firm, or both. Typically, it doesn't cost any more to go through a selection firm because their trading costs are kept low by the sheer volume of their business.

Once hired, the money managers must be monitored by the planner. The planner wants to make sure there isn't a lot of overlap with other managers and that the managers meet their benchmark indexes. If they consistently under perform, they aren't choosing very good stocks and need to be replaced. If they over perform, they may be too aggressive, perhaps using options strategies or buying, say, value when they're supposed to be buying small-cap stocks.

A word about wraps

A "wrap" in financial terms isn't a coat or a fancy sandwich or what movie directors say when they're done filming. Instead, it's an account that combines private management and trade execution.

Available at most brokerage and planning firms, the wrap account usually requires a $100,000 minimum investment. Thus, in order to achieve diversification in seven or eight different asset classes, you'd need at least $700,000 or $800,000. That may make wrap accounts infeasible for many retirees.

A wrap is akin to the asset-management account we've been talking about, except many asset-management accounts are fully diversified at the minimum investment level, usually $150,000. Either a wrap or an asset-management account might be the sort of arrangement that you should consider for your Bucket No. 3.

But more important than what the account is called is what it costs. Wrap accounts too often include some extra costs. Whether yours is a wrap or asset-management account, you'll want to hold the total expense to under 2% annually of the amount invested—that's management fees, trading costs, everything.

And then a final word about integrity

Most financial professionals are highly ethical and responsible. But, of course, they're not immune to the personal frailties that plague other professions. Knowledge is your best safeguard against deception and incompetence.

It'll be up to you to evaluate the planner's performance and assess his advice. You've got to remain alert. It's not enough to say, in effect, "Here's my money. Take good care of it for me." Remember, as long as the cost is reasonable and accountable, it's not how you compensate your advisor that's most important but rather how comfortable you are and whether you are meeting your goals within a stated risk tolerance.

Of course, you shouldn't ever sign a blank document or allow the planner to break the law by signing your name to anything. Don't give him authority to make transactions without your knowledge or consent. Don't agree to list him as joint owner or beneficiary on any of your accounts. And you shouldn't pay more than 50% in advance for planning work or pay for asset management in advance. In fact, I think you should pay quarterly and in arrears for asset management and not be required to pay any sales charges, or loads if you are paying an ongoing fee.

Look out, especially, for any financial professional who promises "a sure thing" or the need to "act quickly before it's too late." There are *no* sure things, and acting quickly without thinking causes many a financial debacle.

And if you become dissatisfied, don't hesitate to change advisors.

Chapter 11

10 More Steps You Can Take to 'Bulletproof' Your Retirement

Short of inheriting a zillion dollars, setting up your *Buckets of Money®* plan is one of the smartest steps you can take to ensure a comfortable retirement. But it's not the only thing.

Whether you're on the threshold of retirement or still decades from it, there's more you can do to pave the way. Achieving financial literacy is a lifelong process, and in this chapter, I want to outline other measures you can take or habits you can foster that'll serve you well in your later years.

Some of these ideas go against the grain, yet there's nothing magical or maybe even startlingly original about most of them. But because you've taken the time and made the effort to grapple with the Buckets philosophy, you may be hungry for other ways to get your financial life in order. If Buckets is the main course, consider these to be financially healthy side dishes that only enhance the enjoyment of the entrée.

1. Start early, save much, live long.

Time creates money. Every so often, you read about somebody who died at age 104 and, despite working only as a dishwasher or a gardener, was able to bequeath maybe a million dollars to a favorite school or charity. Looking closer, you'll find that those folks started saving early, squirreling away their pennies and allowing the miracle of compounding to do its work.

Few investors ever have big sums handed to them via inheritances or gifts. Instead, they accumulate assets by working hard, by doing without, by managing well, and by accepting reasonable risks. All of us can learn from these poor-but-persistent savers.

The first lesson: *You can't start too soon.* In fact, to start saving at an early age is the best way to ensure a comfortable retirement. A 25-year-old who saves just $50 a week will have more than $756,000 by age 65, assuming an 8% tax-deferred return. If that same young person were to delay saving by just 10 years, he or she would accumulate by age 65 only $323,000—134% less.

So the longer you invest, the more you'll reap the rewards. Yet, sad to say, among adults in their late 50s, median savings are less than $10,000.

Second, *be a disciplined saver.* Don't spend your gross salary because, as I like to say, if your outgo exceeds your income, your upkeep will be your downfall. Or, to put it another way: You definitely can make mistakes but you can't make mistakes indefinitely.

What I'd suggest is getting in the habit of "paying yourself" first—that is, writing a check to your savings plan or mutual-fund account *before* you start paying your bills. That'll force you to cut back elsewhere instead of making your future a low priority. Ten percent of your salary might be a good ultimate goal to shoot for when "paying yourself." But you may have to work up to that.

Remember: The average retiree depends on personal savings to provide nearly 18% of his or her retirement income.

While it's true that money talks, the only thing it says to some people is "good-bye." If you're one of those people, then you really need to get in the savings habit.

Third, *live long*. A person who has saved $150,000 at age 60 will, at 7% interest, have $295,000 at age 70, $580,000 at 80, and $1.1 million when he's 90. Each extra decade does wonders for his wealth, if not for his health.

Thus, the surest way to make any portfolio grow faster is to get out of the spending habit, start saving more money earlier . . . and then keep on doing it.

2. Get out of debt, especially credit-card debt.

When I give seminars, I often joke: "A thief stole my wife's credit cards. But I haven't turned him in yet. So far he's charging less than she did!" It gets a laugh, but it's a guilty laugh, closer to the truth than many listeners would wish.

In truth, needless debt is no laughing matter. Consumers rarely fall deeply into debt all at once. Instead, their expenses outpace their income little by little until the amount owed is overwhelming. Often, credit cards are at the root of that bad habit.

Buying more than you can afford to pay off at the end of the month is a double danger. One, it's likely to preclude you from saving any of your income. And two, such debt takes a huge chunk out of your future wealth.

Credit card charges—*surprise!*—are loans with very expensive interest charges. In fact, the average family owes more than $8,000 on credit cards alone. That's ridiculous! Doubly so since credit-card debt is no longer tax-deductible.

Credit cards are an excellent cash-management tool in disciplined hands—you can actually use the bank's money and defer payment for a month. Besides, plastic has become almost a necessity when traveling, and in an emergency, credit cards are wonderful. But put them in non-disciplined hands in a non-emergency, and the results can be disastrous.

About 70% of credit-card users don't pay in full each month. But paying 17% or 18% or more on your outstanding balance is a fool's game. (Not to mention often paying an annual fee on top of that.) That's at least 15% more than you're getting on your savings account. Does that make sense? Or put another way, wouldn't it make more sense to take those savings and pay off the card?

Look at it as an investment. If you pay off your 18% credit card, it's tantamount to *earning* 18%, guaranteed and tax-free. Not a bad move, right?

Other suggestions:

- *Know your card.* Understand the terms. Many card issuers offer low introductory rates. Then after a few months, they raise the rate sharply on some or all of your purchases.
- *Cough up more than the minimum.* If you can't pay off the balance at month's end, try for some damage control by at least sending in more than the minimum payment. Paying only the monthly minimum on a $1,800 balance on an 18% credit card means that it'll take more than 13 years to eliminate that debt.
- *If all else fails . . .* If you absolutely can't find the discipline to pay off your card each month, consider canceling or cutting up your cards. Or failing that, switch to a charge card, like American Express, rather than a credit card; charge cards *must* be paid off each month. Or switch to a debit card, which pays for your purchases by withdrawing money from your bank account at no additional cost to you.

3. Maximize contributions to your 401(k)/pension plan.

Contributing to your employer-sponsored retirement plan—especially if the employer matches your contribution—is as close as you can get to "free" money. If you work for a private firm, that plan is probably a 401(k)—named for the tax code section that created it; at a nonprofit, it may be called a 403(b).

Use it to the fullest extent possible. Why? Because if you belong to a plan that allows you to invest pre-tax dollars and you are in, say, the 28% tax bracket, you in effect make an immediate 28% on your investment—before it even starts to grow! That's because you're not reporting as income the amount you are saving. It's tough to beat that!

In addition, all the earnings from that contribution are tax-deferred, meaning you don't pay taxes until you retire. Plus, many companies "match" your contribution, often 50 cents to your dollar. That's another 50% profit!

Between taxes not paid, taxes deferred, and company matching, this is almost like robbery without a gun! Yet nearly one-third of workers who have access to a plan do *not* contribute to it. *Pul-eez!* Take advantage of it.

With such a plan, you usually get the choice of having your money in one or more of several vehicles. Commonly these include fixed-interest investments (such as CDs or money markets); bond mutual funds; a balanced mutual fund; diversified stock funds including index funds, small-cap funds, and a host of others; or shares of your employer's stock.

Because retirement is a long-term proposition, most investors should use their 401(k) plan as a Bucket No. 3 asset.

However, those who will be in a low-income tax bracket at retirement will want to begin moving some money into a Bucket No. 2 safety account a few years before they retire because it's sometimes better to draw down retirement funds if they can be spent in the lowest income-tax bracket.

Also, a quick note on employer stock: It can make you rich or drive you to the poor house, depending on the your company's performance. Since even the best of companies have had periods in which their stock price dropped by 30%–50% or more, it's wise to limit the amount of company stock in your 401(k) to no more than 25% of the total.

4. Investigate your pension plan.

A pension plan is one in which your employer promises to give you a specific monthly income for life, starting at retirement, or perhaps a lump sum. These are called defined benefit plans. The amount you get depends on your salary, age, number of years with that employer, and other factors.

Fewer than one-half of retirees receive income from a pension plan, a figure that's been declining because of the growth of the self-employed, temporary, and part-time workforce and because of the popularity of the 401(k). But if you're eligible for a pension, you need to learn the specifics.

Because the plan and its formula are different at every company, it's important to find out, for example, about the vesting schedule (how many years of service before you become partially or fully eligible), what happens if you quit your job, and what the pension plan is invested in and how financially sound is the plan. Also check on how much you can expect to receive, say, at age 60, 62, or 65. Find out what the benefits are for your survivor if you die and whether there is a cost-of-living adjustment.

When you do retire, you'll probably be offered a single-life annuity (a monthly income for life but which stops at your death) or a joint and survivor annuity (a smaller amount that continues as long as either you or your spouse is alive.) Most workers chose the latter. But *should* they?

In effect, by choosing the joint and survivor annuity you're buying a life insurance policy for your surviving spouse. The cost of such a "policy" is the difference between the pay out of the two benefit plans—usually several hundred dollars per month. If you already have sufficient life insurance to cover your survivor's needs, you may be better off taking the single-life annuity. Or with part of the additional income you'll get by not taking the survivor benefit, you can buy your own insurance policy rather than having the company do it for you.

Doing so brings other advantages besides being possibly cheaper: You can get a lump sum from the insurance instead of a monthly check that a pension plan provides. And you can change the beneficiary as well as leave some of the proceeds to heirs, neither of which is possible with the pension plan.

Again, careful attention must be paid to any decision relating to pension distributions, lump sums, cost-of-living adjustments (COLAs), and the like. This is all the more reason to hire a good financial planner.

5. Do something about your estate.

"Estate" sounds so high falutin', like something only somebody like Bill Gates might have. But, in truth, everybody has one, even if it's just a undernourished bank account and a ratty, old car. Your estate is just what you own minus what you owe. And the purpose of estate planning is to answer the questions: Who gets what? And under what conditions?

Estate planning can help ensure that your money and other assets go to the people you want—not those determined by state law. Further, it allows you to divide your assets in such a way as to provide for efficient money management, create the fewest possible legal hassles for your survivors, and possibly minimize the tax bite.

To do this, you first want to figure out what your assets are and how much you want to pass on to heirs. Then come up with a plan that takes into account probate (the legal process that distributes your estate) and estate taxes, which are transfer taxes that can take a big chunk out of your estate if it's over $675,000. That limit will be raised over the next few years, and then the estate tax is totally repealed in the year 2010. (In 2011 the law is destined to revert back to the rules in existence in 2001. Go figure!)

To do even a halfway decent job of this, you're probably going to need the help of professionals, such as an estate-planning lawyer and a certified financial planner.

Some of the issues you may want to discuss include:

- *Writing a will.* Having a will streamlines the process. If you die without having written a will, the state government will provide a standard one according to its laws, and that may be something quite different than what you intended. Do you really want the state making decisions such as who will raise your kids and who will get your money?

    But you don't want just *any* will. You want one tailored for you with some thought, not just a fill-in-the-blanks standard form. Will-writing software programs are cheap but spending a little bit with a lawyer is usually a much better idea. One of the biggest flaws of a one-size-fits-all will is that many times named heirs are able to receive assets without restrictions. But often restrictions are needed.

    For instance, do you want to be sure your 20-year-old spends his inheritance on college, not on a sports car? Are you confident your grandchild will be a good steward of his inheritance and will invest it as wisely? Or should a bank or trust company watch over the assets until he or she is more capable? Do you want to be sure an ex-spouse doesn't walk away with assets you intended for your grandkids? All of this can be accomplished with properly drafted wills and trusts.

- *What stays out of the will?* All wills must be validated by a probate court. This takes time, can cost attorney's fees, and is a public (not a private) process. So most people prefer to avoid probate as much as possible. Ways to do that include titling many assets jointly and/or setting up a living trust. (See below.) When a person dies, some assets—such as joint accounts and those that name a beneficiary, like life insurance and IRAs—go immediately to the co-owner or to the named beneficiary. Everything else is passed to the heirs according to the will.

- *Setting up a living trust.* This is a popular way of seeing that other assets, such as your home, bank accounts, and brokerage accounts, are kept out of probate. A big advantage is that although you've placed assets in trust, you can name yourself as trustee and keep control over them until you die, when the assets then pass immediately to your beneficiaries.

    Among a living trust's many advantages are that it's nearly impossible to challenge and it's valid throughout the United States, unlike wills. Further, most people opt for a *revocable* living trust, meaning they can change or cancel the trust arrangement at any point during their lifetime. Even if you have a living trust, you probably should still have a will.

    A couple important points: First, a trust is really just a container, an envelope of sorts. It has no intrinsic value and no worth until and unless you re-title assets into the trust. Otherwise, all that legal effort is fruitless. Second, it avoids probate but not taxes. Your heirs will get their legacy sooner than they otherwise would, but they still may need to pay taxes on it if the estate exceeds the tax-free limits.

- *The role of multiple trusts.* A comprehensive estate plan may consist of several trusts. These can be set up for a number of different purposes. To cite just a few:
  —Generation-skipping trusts allow income from your trust to be used by your children, although some or all of the principal passes to your grandchildren.
  —Bypass trusts (also called "AB" or "Martial Life Estate" trusts) provide for your spouse upon your death. But then the trust assets pass tax-free to the trust's final beneficiaries (usually your kids) upon your spouse's death.
  —QTIP (Qualified Terminable Interest Property) trusts ensure your surviving spouse gets income but that the assets eventually go to your children, not to a new spouse of your former husband or wife.
  —Charitable remainder trusts permit you to contribute assets to a charity and get a tax deduction as well as an annuity from the income.
- *Including a living will.* A living will, usually part of a living trust, declares your preference for medical treatment if you become seriously ill. It often is accompanied by a *durable power of attorney for health care,* which appoints an adult to have legal authority to make medical decisions for you if you become incapacitated. A living will has nothing to do with a regular will, which divides property.

- *Including a durable power of attorney for financial matters.* Similar to the durable power of attorney for health care, this one allows you to name someone to handle your money if you cannot. This can avoid prolonged, costly court proceedings if you become incapacitated.
- *Gifting.* Another way of avoiding taxes—or shifting taxes to someone in a lower tax bracket—is giving away some of your assets while you're still alive. Most gifts are by older people to their children and grand-children with an eye to helping them buy a house or get an education. Each year, you can give up to $10,000 ($20,000 from a married couple) to each family member or heir without gift or estate taxes. (By contrast, if the money stays in your estate, the tax at death could be as much as 55%.) If you have the cash flow and plan far enough ahead, you can avoid much in estate taxes through this strategy.

As you can see, there are lots of possibilities. What's more, estate plans require periodic review and revision if they are to stay current and viable, especially if your marital status changes, you change your state of residence, or your health or income changes.

6. Pay off your mortgage—*maybe!*

Owning the family home free and clear is a goal of the mortgage-burdened everywhere. They dream of not having to write that check every month, and that's a worthy objective. But is it the best possible solution for everyone?

Certainly it would feel great to be freed from your mortgage. But wouldn't it feel even better to have the mortgage taken care of but still get that important tax deduction?

If you're able to save to send in extra payments in hopes of paying off your home loan early, maybe you could put some or all of that money to work in a smarter way—say, a Roth IRA. Withdrawals from a Roth (named for a U.S. Senator from Delaware who sponsored the legislation) are tax-free, provided you leave the money in the account for at least five years after making the first contribution and you're over 59½. (A Roth IRA doesn't require you to begin making withdrawals by 70½ or to stop making contributions after that age as does the traditional IRA.)

So with the money that you'd otherwise use to make extra loan payments, you could build up a Roth and get a tax-free nut with which to pay down the loan. Yes, you'd still need to write that check each month to the bank or savings and loan. But if you knew the tax-free source from which the money was coming—and you kept what's likely your biggest tax deduction—wouldn't it be worth it? Think about it.

7. Do some straight thinking about life insurance.

There's an awful lot of confusion about insurance in general. But here's the bedrock truth: *The aim of all insurance is to protect against the risk of financial loss.* The aim for most individuals isn't necessarily to make money from their insurance or to protect against emotional loss (which is impossible), but rather find the least expensive solution to the need for protection.

Folks rarely complain when they make it through another year without collecting on their life insurance. But they do complain that they don't understand insurance. Indeed, the mechanics and the nomenclature—*term, whole, universal, variable,* and the like—can be confusing.

What's even more confusing is some of the misinformation that is occasionally doled out by the financial press, talking heads, and sometimes even the insurance industry itself. My advice: Unless you are in a high tax bracket or have surplus cash to invest beyond your retirement plans and Roth IRA, buy life insurance not as an investment but for protection against financial loss—like dying and leaving your dependents without a breadwinner.

To cover such a loss, you should buy the cheapest form of term life insurance. For certain individuals it may actually be cheaper in the long run to buy a permanent policy, especially if they overfund it and build up a significant cash value. That way, in the later years when term insurance is very expensive, the permanent policy may have accumulated enough equity to cover the long-term cost of the mortality expense. Variable life policies allow the cash value to be invested in sub accounts like stock mutual funds, and the mortality expense is withdrawn tax-free from the earnings. It's like buying term insurance and investing the difference in a tax-sheltered environment.

As a general rule, those with limited cash flow and a high need for temporary coverage should buy term insurance. Those in high tax brackets who either can't qualify for Roth IRAs or are already funding them may want to consider permanent insurance like variable universal life. In most cases a combination of the two—term and permanent—makes the most sense: term for your short-term needs and permanent for long-term needs and supplemental, tax-favored savings.

It's important to evaluate your particular situation before deciding which type or types of life insurance work best for you. This is yet another area in which a solid financial planner can help.

8. Know what else you need to protect against.

As you approach your retirement years, ask yourself: What are my biggest potential financial losses ? Well, your house could burn down, your job could disappear, or through injury or illness, you could become unable to take care of yourself.

You probably already have fire insurance, and you might be able to replace your job. But what if you lost your ability to produce an income? Or, if you're not working, what if you were forced to enter a nursing home? Either would qualify as a major financial reversal, the kind that insurance is best designed for.

So you should also consider:

Disability insurance. If you become sick or injured and can't work, that's when big trouble begins. You could lose your home, your ability to put your kids through school, your shot at building a retirement nest-egg. After all, medical advances can keep you alive in cases where you would have died a generation ago—but that doesn't mean you won't be devastated by the costs and by the loss of income.

Disability insurance *is* expensive. But guess why: Because there's a good chance you're going to need to file a claim. In fact, insurers figure that you're five times more likely to be disabled than to die during your working life. Of course, if you weren't likely to need it, the policy would be cheap. But is that a reason not to have it? I don't think so.

Be very careful when buying disability insurance. Do a lot of research and compare and contrast policies on such points as the definition of disability, the waiting period (known as the "elimination" period)—i.e., how long after being disabled before you get the benefits; monthly income; cost-of-living adjustments; what kind or amount of work you may continue to do, if able; and the "integration," or how the policy meshes with other benefits or income you receive.

Long-term care insurance. While disability insurance is important for the non-retired, the big issue for retirees becomes long-term care insurance. LTCI is a question you could someday face for yourself . . . and maybe even sooner for your parents. Today's extended life spans have upped the odds of suffering heart attacks, cancer, strokes, or Alzheimer's disease. Even a broken hip or a bout of pneumonia can devour decades of savings in a matter of months if you need home health care or need to be admitted to a long-term care facility. So LTCI is a good way of avoiding a terrible cash drain in your retirement years.

More than half the women and about a third of men who reach age 65 will spend some time in a nursing home. And it ain't cheap, running in the $40,000-to-$60,000-a-year range—and neither private health insurance nor Medicare pays for it. So unless you're very wealthy, this should be a priority.

The cost of LTCI is directly related to your age, so there's an advantage in buying it early (because it'll be cheaper), but probably not too early (because you'll be paying premiums to guard against a very unlikely event.) So late middle age, say, your 50s or early 60s, is probably the optimal time.

The policy should contain benefits that will pay for care wherever you'll likely to need it: at home, in adult day care, assisted living, or a nursing home. It also should include inflation protection. Your state insurance department sets the standards for this type of policy, and you might want to check with that agency, or with a an advisor who specializes in LTCI, before you buy.

Once purchased, the cost of the policy usually remains the same for life. (Even wealthy folks often buy LTCI because, while they could afford long-term care, they'd rather spend a few hundred dollars a year on a policy than expend their assets on the care itself and thus, short-change their heirs.)

So, LTCI is worth thinking about, especially when you're young enough to afford it and your health is good enough to qualify for it.

9. Level with your (adult) kids.

You owe it to your children—and to yourself—to be more forthcoming about money than your parents probably were with you. Just telling your kids "everything is taken care of" isn't enough. After all, they may be forced to make vital health-care choices without understanding what kind of insurance you have, to take care of your house and car without knowing the name of your insurance agent, and to pay bills without even being sure of where you keep the checkbook. What's more, if they are likely to inherit some money—or *not* inherit any—that's information that would be very helpful to them for planning purposes.

Poor parent-child communication can cause big money problems. A worst-case scenario: The parent could have a major stroke without having authorized a power of attorney. Thus, even the children do not have the legal authority to pay his/her bills or file the parent's taxes. The children might even need to seek a court-appointed conservator, a difficult process that could run up huge legal fees.

Why is it so hard for the generations to talk? Discussing death and disability isn't a million laughs, and such a discussion reminds us of an unwanted change in the relationship. The parents feel old, and signing a power of attorney feels like losing control. Plus, many adult children don't feel competent themselves when it comes to money.

Nonetheless, such talks are absolutely necessary. Most people, if they get up the nerve at all, wait until parents are old and frail. But the best time to have a financial dialogue is when parents are, say, in their 50s or at the latest in their 60s.

You should make sure your kids know:

- Where you store your financial records, including tax returns, pension information, and investment data.
- What kind of medical insurance you have.
- Who your doctors are and what kind of medications you take.
- The status of your estate planning, including wills and trusts.
- Who is the executor of your will.
- How you would expect to handle the costs of an extended illness.

- Where your emergency paperwork is kept, including powers of attorney, will, living wills, trusts, etc.
- Your monthly income and expenses.
- How you plan to divide your assets.
- The names, addresses, and phone numbers of all your advisors, including estate lawyer, accountant, investment advisors, trust officers, insurance agent, banker, and the like.

10. Never forget that investing is a marathon, not a sprint.

Even with all the market's dips and dives, the odds still favor investors who diversify and keep their money long-term in stocks. Your *Buckets of Money*® philosophy should be a powerful inducement to long-term thinking.

I know I've said this before. In fact, it's a theme of this book, but it bears repeating: To be successful in your retirement planning, you've got to think long-term. The average Wall Street investor is a sprinter who looks for the best possible short-term return. But you're a marathoner. You seek long-term results. This philosophy may give you short-run pain from time to time but, with any kind of luck, it will give you long-run joy.

Your goal is to build a winning, long-term portfolio. To do so, try to:

- *Stay firmly focused on the future.* Remind yourself not to be too concerned about whether the market is up or down today, whether the Fed will/will not lower or raise interest rates, whether the Street likes or hates the newest crop of presidential contenders.

Instead, ask yourself if the long-term prospects for the U.S. economy are solid and whether the long-term prospects for American business and industry are good. Know that good times are always alloyed with bad, that in the last half century there have been 14 bear markets (occurring roughly every 3.5 years), and, further, that four wars, nine recessions, eight presidents, and one impeachment since World War II didn't keep profits from going up 55-fold and the stock market up 60-times.

- *Avoid panic.* Obsessively watching CNBC or CNNfn can leave you with the impression of an impending Armageddon or lead you to believe you can get rich quick. But the truth is that compulsively watching even the best financial networks or reading even the top financial newspapers or magazines can be a little bit like trying to tell the time by looking only at the second hand of your watch. Instead, be a long-term investor who makes rational, informed decisions and accepts a certain amount of volatility as a fact of financial life. People who think logically are a nice contrast to the rest of the world, and as a result, they likely will prosper.

- *Be committed to investing in equities.* Lack of patience is probably the single, biggest obstacle to successful stock-market investing. When there's a downturn, don't think about how much you've lost—think about how many more shares you can now purchase for the same amount of money. Successful long-term investors see downturns, painful as they are, as buying opportunities.

- *Guard against overconfidence.* The ancient law of investing—"Be fearful when others are greedy and greedy when others are fearful"—is still in effect. Excessive hubris is one of the biggest threats to any investor. Remember, you don't need market-beating returns to do well. Just matching, or nearly matching, the market over a period of time will probably be just fine.

- *Keep diversified.* Hot stocks, hot sectors, hot styles of investing come and go like summer squalls. The successful, long-term investor is he who invests broadly, re-balances, and stays invested in both bearish and bullish periods.

- *Get right with risk.* Extra risk may lead to extra returns—but it's not guaranteed. On the other hand, to get extra returns, you *do* have to take extra risk. So develop a comfort level that works for you, and stick to it.

- *Know the long-term trend is your friend.* The Baby Boomers—that huge demographic wave that's entering middle age—need the stock market for funding both their retirement and their children's education. So it's very likely they will continue to pour available savings into stocks. By and large, these are savvy, long-term players better informed than investors in the past and more likely to remain calmer during downturns. In addition, Boomers will receive over $10 trillion from their parents in the next 15 to 20 years. Where else will that go long-term but into equities, the stock market and real estate?

So, if you want a comfortable retirement, you've got to be willing to take some risks with equity investments, spend less, save more, and continue to educate yourself in the ins and outs of modern financial planning. This isn't, as the saying goes, rocket science. But it does take some thought and some effort. Or as someone once noted: Success is a matter of luck—just ask any failure.

Whew! That's it. That's all the advice I can muster for now. After all, I'm not young enough to know everything. But I have told you a great deal that I've learned in almost three decades of being a financial advisor. Except for one, overarching and not inconsequential, suggestion in the next chapter.

Chapter 12

ENJOYING LIFE AS A 'BUCKETEER'

"Money is better than poverty, if only for financial reasons," Woody Allen once said, and he's right. All things being equal, it's better to be rich than poor. But as we know, all things aren't equal, and I want to end this book with what I hope is a bit of perspective.

For many pages now I've talked about how to make your retirement financially secure. Obviously, that's important *up to a point*. But if you get too far beyond that point, if you get to where the digits, decimal points, and dollar signs obscure life's other joys, you've gone too far.

Making money for people, managing people's money is my calling, my livelihood, my passion. There's nothing I'd rather be doing as an occupation. But I'd be lying if I told you it was the most important thing in the world for me as I roll out of bed in the morning. For me, that most important thing is family. My wife Jeanne and our kids and my extended family are at the center of my solar system. Money is just how I earn my living and keep those planets spinning.

I sometimes reflect on the words of Charlie Munger, Warren Buffet's sidekick: "If all you succeed in doing in life is getting rich by buying little pieces of paper, it's a failed life," he said. "Life is more than being shrewd in wealth accumulation." I couldn't agree more.

The variety of riches

Money is a two-edged sword. It's been called the root of all evil. And that's probably true. But it's a fact that money is the root of a lot of other things, too. And, by golly, a man needs roots.

So, yes, you need money to retire and I hope *Buckets of Money*® will make that possible in abundance. But you also need engagement and connection with people and pursuits. If you're never rich in anything but friends, family, and worthwhile things to do, you're still pretty rich.

We all recognize that some people get more joy out of life than others do. The same is true in retirement. This joy doesn't correlate with how much money you have. It correlates, I believe, with how *involved* you are. Involved with your family, friends, country, planet. Involved with trying to make life better for others. Involved with physical activity and mental stimulation. Involved with romantic love. Involved with pets and grandchildren and the PTA and woodworking and model-airplane flying and raising roses or anything-else-that-interests-you.

Interest. That's the key. And I don't just mean simple or compound interest. I mean your degree of interest in the world around you. There's no substitute for that.

What's money mean to you?

You probably won't have as much money in retirement as you did when working. Thus, it's important to understand what money means to you—to sort out your fiscal priorities, to break what's probably a family code of silence about money, and come to grips with your money attitudes. That can be a chore but a liberation, too.

Does your attitude toward money help you lead an emotionally healthy life or does it represent an obstacle to achieving that? Do you rule money or does money rule you? Ruling money means knowing what your priorities are, knowing what you're ready to give up, knowing what are acceptable tradeoffs.

Much of this book has been aimed at trying to help you stave off fears about retirement, fears that you won't have enough money. I hope I've helped you allay those concerns. But I also want to make the point that money should represent freedom and an expanded lust for life, not just security. Being successful in the retirement game doesn't mean becoming the richest guy in the cemetery. It means living as richly as possible the latter third or so of your life.

A lot of us give lip service to the idea that accumulating money now will allow us later to do what we really want to do. And that's true. But not if we keep postponing forever what it is we really want to do. Living well doesn't always depend on having more money or more things.

Here's the ultimate question: What do you want to do with the rest of your life? Start a business? Write a novel? Visit each of the national parks? Work for charities? Help save the environment? Or just play lots of golf?

What's your personal vision of how the world could be improved? What causes could you serve, injustices could you correct, dreams could you fulfill?

And how are you situated to reach those goals? What are your unique needs and talents? What more do you need to learn and how do you need to grow before you can have a realistic shot at attaining your objectives? How can you best contribute to others? What have you learned in life that's worth passing along?

I urge you to take the time to think about questions like those and act upon the answers. I believe you'll find out you're surrounded by opportunities. Even if you're not going to retire with a small fortune, there is much to be done for yourself and others.

No safety in numbers

Our culture has come to accept great wealth as a personal value. But, in my view, life is so short, and there is no safety in numbers or anything else. So my advice would be: Don't let your wealth, or your pursuit of wealth, blind you or shield you from life.

Sure, save. Invest. Use your head to make your money go as far as you can. But don't let money, or lack of it, keep you from jumping on life's carousel. In short, living well doesn't always depend on having more money. Needs and expenses have an amazing ability to keep pace with income. So you can decide to make more . . . or you can decide to need less.

Whatever you decide, try to see your money as a tool of liberation, not a financial ball and chain. A common mistake many people make is not paying enough attention to their finances. But you also can pay *too* much attention. We regret more things we didn't do than those we did. And as others have said, the best things in life aren't things.

For a final word on the subject, I defer to Henrik Ibsen, the playwright, who wrote: "Money may be the husk of many things, but not the kernel. It brings you food, but not appetite; medicine but not health; acquaintances, but not friends; servants, but not faithfulness; days of joy, but not peace or happiness."

Go forth, enjoy and prosper!

Appendix A
RECOMMENDED BOOKS

Jonathan Clements, 25 MYTHS TO AVOID—IF YOU WANT TO MANAGE YOUR MONEY RIGHT: *The New Rules for Financial Success* (New York: Fireside/Simon & Schuster, 1998)

Harry S. Dent, Jr., THE GREAT BOOM AHEAD: *Your Comprehensive Guide to Personal and Business Profit in the New Era of Prosperity* (New York: Hyperion, 1993)

———, THE ROARING 2000s: *Building the Wealth and Lifestyle You Desire in the Greatest Boom in History* (New York: Simon & Schuster, 1998)

Nancy Dunnan, DUN & BRADSTREET GUIDE TO YOUR INVESTMENTS, 1999 (HarperPerennial, 1999).

Ric Edelman, THE NEW RULES OF MONEY (Harper-Collins, 1998).

————, THE TRUTH ABOUT MONEY, 2nd edn. (Harper-Business, 1998).

Jordan Goodman, DICTIONARY OF FINANCE AND INVESTMENT TERMS, 5th edn. (Barrons Educational Series, 1998).

————, EVERYONE'S MONEY BOOK, 3rd edn. (Dearborn Trade, 2001).

Gary L. Klott, THE NEW YORK TIMES COMPLETE GUIDE TO PERSONAL INVESTING (Times Books, 1987).

Lynn O'Shaughnessy, THE RETIREMENT BIBLE (Hungry Minds, 2001).

Barbara Stanny, PRINCE CHARMING ISN'T COMING; HOW WOMEN GET SMART ABOUT MONEY (Viking, 1997).

Ralph Warner, GET A LIFE: YOU DON'T NEED A MILLION TO RETIRE WELL (Nolo, 1996).

Appendix B
HELPFUL ONLINE SITES

Here are just a few of the hundreds, if not thousands, of helpful web sites. Many of these allow you to track your investments as well as learn about personal finance and follow financial news.

www.bucketsofmoney.com

My website that offers various educational materials to assist with your Buckets planning, including worksheets, calculators, and this *Buckets of Money®* hard-back book and booklet. Or locate an advisor in your area, check my seminar schedule, and order my monthly newsletter.

www.24-7financial.com

A comprehensive consumer financial website with articles, Q&A, message boards, calculators, financial planning tools and offering P.U.R.E. fee-only plans. (Personalized. Unbiased. Reputable. Exemplary.)

www.abcnews.go.com/sections/business
This ABC News site has news, features, and personal-finance tools.

www.collegeparents.org
A private membership organization aimed at helping parents cope with college expenses.

www.marketwatch.com
This site, similar to ABC's, is operated by the CBS network.

www.money.com
The site, run by CNN and *Money* magazine, includes general financial and budgeting information as well as several calculators for help in making financial decisions.

http://moneycentral.msn.com
This one, run by Microsoft, also includes news and personal-finance information as well as a search mechanism for finding financial planners.

www.moneyzone.com
Oriented more toward entrepreneurs, this site includes businesses for sale as well as funding opportunities.

www.morningstar.com
The definitive site for mutual-fund information.

www.napfa.org and **www.fpanet.org**
These professional organizations provide search mechanisms to allow you to find financial planners who practice near you.

www.sec.gov and **www.nasd.com**

These governmental or quasi-governmental agencies keep records on brokers, planners, and other financial professionals.

About the Author

Raymond J. Lucia, CFP™, a financial planner since 1974, manages more than $500 million in client assets. His nationally-syndicated talk show, "The Ray Lucia Show," reaches hundreds of thousands of listeners daily and continues to grow in popularity. He lives in San Diego, where he heads the Raymond J. Lucia Companies, Inc. and is also chief executive officer of 24-7financial.

A nationally renowned expert in the field of financial and business management, Ray was named by *Radio and Records* magazine as one of its "Rising Stars of 2001" for his entertaining and informative radio shows. His show has been described as a clinic on personal finance that covers a wide range of issues and provides a forum for listeners everywhere.

Dale Fetherling has written, edited, or co-authored a dozen non-fiction books and taught writing and editing at five colleges and universities. He's based in San Diego.